ROOTS OF AMERICA

An Anthology of Documents
relating to
American History
in the
West Sussex Record Office
Chichester, England

Edited by
Kim C. Leslie

Published by

THE WEST SUSSEX COUNTY COUNCIL
COUNTY HALL, CHICHESTER, ENGLAND
1976

to commemorate
the Bicentenary of American Independence

The documents and books
referred to in this anthology
are open for inspection at
The West Sussex Record Office,
County Hall, Chichester,
from Mondays to Fridays
from 9.15 a.m. to 12.30 p.m.
and 1.30 p.m. to 5.00 p.m.,
except on Bank Holidays, Good Fridays and
any other days appointed as Public Holidays.

Cover illustration
Waterfront view of Portland, Maine, 1859
(West Sussex Record Office, Lyons Papers)

Contents

	page
Preface	v
First Settlements	1
Colonial Troubles	6
The War of Independence	17
Aftermath of War: the Need for Unity	24
'Free Trade and Sailors' Rights': War with Britain Again	26
'If you want to live, come here': Emigration to the United States	32
Slavery	49
The Civil War	54
Englishmen in America	77
Appendix: Sussex and America	97
Index	108

Preface

A great deal of American history remains to be written from original documentation preserved in archive repositories throughout Great Britain. That these collections are extensive and contain a large amount of material hitherto unknown to scholars has been amply demonstrated by B. R. Crick and Miriam Alman in their *Guide to Manuscripts Relating to America in Great Britain and Ireland*.[1]

The American story told in the following pages has been compiled around manuscript and printed material in the custody of the West Sussex Record Office at Chichester, the great majority of which was unrecorded by Crick and Alman.[2] Their survey was made nearly twenty years ago and since then much new material has been accessioned and made available at the West Sussex Record Office.

The selections made for this anthology are now being published as a small contribution towards the celebration of the Bicentenary of American Independence in 1976. Covering a wide range of subject matter from colonial to republican times—including relations with the Indians, religious missions, emigration from England and Ireland, slavery, some travel diaries, the two wars with Great Britain and the shattering conflict of the Civil War which nearly led to a third—the story presented here in no way claims to be either definitive or comprehensive. It is more an attempt to bring to the public notice something of the richness and variety of the American story in just one of the many provincial record offices in England. The story has been woven together with a series of introductory narratives and background notes, and in a few cases with extracts taken from 18th century volumes of *The Gentleman's Magazine*.

The links between Sussex and America have been legion. 'The *first* President, George Washington, had Sussex connections. From Sussex families went forth a *first* and *last* Imperial governor to America, and other governors; on its soil was drafted the *first* state constitution of Pennsylvania, by William Penn, who lived in Sussex and there found a Sussex bride, as did John Harvard, founder of the *first* American University, to which a Sussex family gave its *first* treasurer, Herbert Pelham; in its county town, Lewes, lived Thomas Paine, prime moving spirit in the *first* American civil war, which became the War of Independence. George Percy, one of the *first* Virginian settlers, and a President of Virginia before the advent of Lord De La Warr, its *first* governor, was a Sussex man, as were Lord De La Warr and Peter Pelham, *first* artist resident in and producer of the *first* mezzotint plate ever prepared in America . . . One of the *first* graduates of Harvard College, John Allin . . . became vicar of Rye, in Sussex. In the same ancient town lived and wrote for eighteen years that unparalleled American, Henry James . . . In Sussex churches tombs and brasses are to be found engraved with names that grow as cities grow, embedded indestructibly in their fame . . .'[3] A Sussex church and a Sussex mansion have been faithfully copied in California and

---

[1] Published for the British Association for American Studies by the Oxford University Press (1961). A revision is in preparation (March 1976).

[2] Of the documents referred to in this anthology, their *Guide* only made reference to the Lyons Papers and to the Petworth House Archives.

[3] David McLean, 'Sussex and the U.S.A.' in *Sussex County Magazine*, vol. 4 (1930), p. 47.

Rhode Island, and high on the Sussex Downs is the tower of Vandalia, the monument to the speculative Grand Ohio Company which failed in the late 18th century. Many of the links are as surprising as they are numerous. A selection of these places with American connections has been listed as an appendix to this anthology, hopefully to serve as a brief guide for those making their own American pilgrimage in Sussex.

The production of this anthology has been made possible through the several owners of the documents who have so generously made them available through the West Sussex Record Office where they are deposited.[1] For permission to use them here grateful thanks are extended to His Grace the Duke of Norfolk (the Lyons Papers); Lord Cowdray (the Cowdray Archives); Lord Egremont (the Petworth House Archives); the Trustees of Dunford House (the Cobden Papers); the Trustees of the Goodwood Estate (the Goodwood Archives); the Trustees of the Edward James Foundation (the West Dean Archives); Mrs. E. Fuller (the Fuller Collection); Miss E. Johnstone (the Hawkins Papers); Mr. G. Stanhope-Lovell (the Badcock Papers); Major and Mrs. J. M. Maxse (the Maxse Papers); the clergy and churchwardens of Aldingbourne, West Chiltington, West Grinstead, Lindfield and Lyminster. A very special debt of acknowledgement is due to the President of New England College, Henniker, New Hampshire, and the Director of the British Campus, Arundel, who have so very generously contributed towards covering the cost of the illustrations. Through this kindness yet one more link has been forged between Sussex and America in this bicentenary year.

My sincere thanks are also due to Mrs. Marjorie Hallam, Mr. E. W. Holden, Dr. Peter Martin and Mrs. Stella Palmer, as well as to the Cultural Attaché of the American Embassy in London, and the staff of the Reference Department of the West Sussex County Library Service, Chichester, and H. M. Customs and Excise Library Services, London. Colleagues at the Record Office, Stephen Freeth, Alison and Timothy McCann, Alan Readman and Peter Wilkinson, have all borne my frequent pleas for help in unravelling the mysteries of atrocious 19th century handwriting with long-suffering patience. Above all I am indebted to Mrs. Patricia Gill, County Archivist for West Sussex, for every help and encouragement in making the whole production possible, and to my wife, Jennifer, who has helped prepare the typescript, offered many suggestions and given so much support throughout all stages of the work.

Finally, a note about the edited text. All original spellings have been retained throughout, but in some cases punctuation has been modified to make for greater clarity. Certain writers have underlined words in their manuscripts; this has been indicated here by the use of italics.

Kim C. Leslie
West Sussex Record Office
March 1976

---

[1] Note, however, that the Petworth House Archives continue to be stored at Petworth House, although in the custody of the West Sussex Record Office. All requests to make use of these archives must be made direct to the County Archivist.

First Settlements

The first permanent English settlements in North America were carved from the barren wilderness of the Atlantic seaboard in the early 17th century. The new settlers came seeking profitable adventure and new trading opportunities, others for a small plot of land they could call their own, others came searching for the religious freedom they were denied in Europe.

Fighting disease and starvation and the ever present menace of the surrounding Indians, these early settlers were tested to the limits of human endurance. At Jamestown, Virginia—first of the successful English settlements—four-fifths of the settlers died between 1607 and 1624. 'The winning of a beachhead in Virginia cost far more casualties, in proportion to numbers engaged, than did the conquest of any of the Japanese-held Islands in World War II . . . "Doggs, catts, ratts, and mice" were esteemed delicasies and boiled shoes became a regular article of diet . . . Of the 500 men and women living in Jamestown in October, 1609, only 60 were alive in April, 1610.'[1] To the North, at Plymouth Plantation, the Puritans faced hostility whichever way they looked: '. . . they had now no friends to welcome them nor inns to entertain or refresh their weatherbeaten bodies; no houses or much less towns to repair to, to seek for succour . . . If they looked behind them, there was the mighty ocean which they had passed and was now as a main bar and gulf to separate them from all the civil parts of the world . . . What could now sustain them but the Spirit of God and his grace? . . .'[2]

These early colonials came seeking freedom, and out of their determination for self-government was forged the foundation of America's democratic institutions, two centuries at least before there was anything comparable elsewhere in the world. The Virginian Assembly of 1619 was the first popularly-elected legislative body in the New World, whilst the Mayflower Compact, made the following year between the Puritan Pilgrim Fathers, established the understanding that government was to be based upon the will of the majority. By '1660 New England, Virginia, and Maryland were already full-fledged commonwealths possessing most of the apparatus of civilized life as developed up to that time, reproducing or attempting to improve on the institutions of the homeland, yet conscious of their peculiar interests and capable of defending themselves against any foreign enemy. Utopia was still far off, but the essential nuclei of the American Republic were already formed'.[3]

---

[1] John C. Miller, *The First Frontier: Life in Colonial America* (1966), pp. 15, 22.
[2] S. E. Morison (ed.), *William Bradford of Plymouth Plantation, 1620–1647* (1959), pp. 61–63.
[3] Samuel Eliot Morison & Henry Steele Commager, *The Growth of the American Republic*, vol. 1 (5th edn. 1962), p. 72.

i   New Netherland

The first English settlers were soon followed by the Dutch. For some forty years—between 1624 and 1664—they planted their own colony of New Netherland along the eastern seaboard, driving a wedge between Virginia and New England, a threat and a barrier to English colonial expansion.

The Dutch conquest was celebrated by the Dutch map-maker, Nicolas Visscher. His decorative map of the eastern seaboard, complete with a waterfront panorama of New Amsterdam, although undated, was produced sometime between 1638 and 1664.

The first settlers arrived in 1624 with a commercial grant made by the Dutch West India Company. Manhattan Island was purchased from the Indians and New Amsterdam established as a trading-post chiefly for furs and as a base for the Dutch tobacco trade with Virginia. From Manhattan, settlements were driven north and north-eastwards up the Hudson and Connecticut valleys, and south-westwards towards the Delaware, guarded by Dutch military forts.

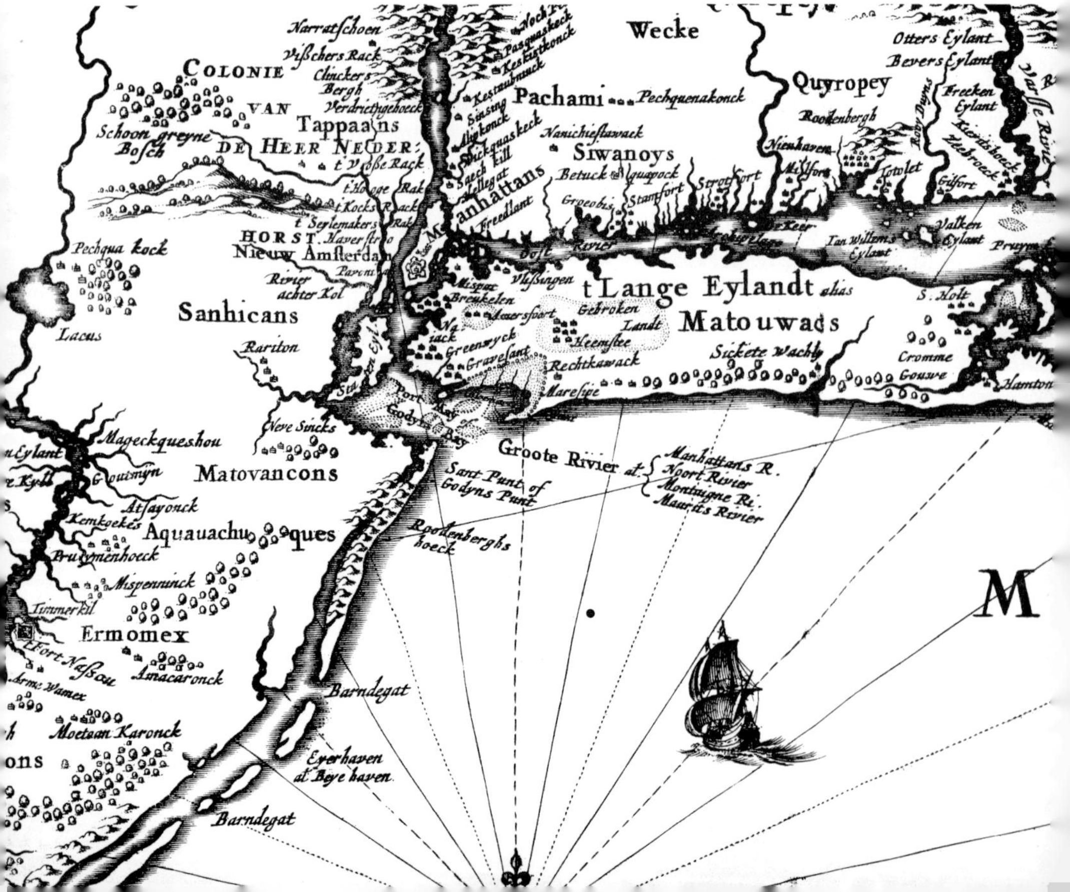

Fig. 1

To the English the Dutch were intruders. Friction became intense. Disregarding the Dutch presence, Charles II granted his brother James, Duke of York, a vast tract of land between Connecticut and the Delaware—otherwise Dutch property! By the 1660s, after years of neglect and maladministration, the West India Company bankrupt, governor Peter Stuyvesant surrendered without bloodshed. In honour of the new English proprietor, New Amsterdam became New York and the vast Dutch hinterland was carved up to create New York and New Jersey.

Present day America still bears witness to the Dutch presence of the 17th century. Districts such as Harlem (Haerlem) and Brooklyn (Breukelen) in New York, the vestiges of Dutch law in New York State, and families such as Vanderbilt and Roosevelt have left the indelible mark of this short-lived Dutch administration in North America.

For another section of this map see plate no. I.   *Petworth House Archives 3843.*

ii   'The Natives are very vile people . . .'

According to many early writers, colonial expansion in America was the working of God's purpose as the means of converting a 'very vile people, horrible Idolaters' to the ways of English Christianity. This was the view of the author of *A Prospect of the Most Famous Parts of the World* . . . published in London in 1646 'for William Humble, and . . . to be sold at his shop in Popes-head Palace'.

'. . . God in these latter times hath enlarged our possessions, that his Gospel might be propagated, and hath discovered to us Inhabitants almost in every corner of the earth . . . And West-ward to the utmost parts of *America* . . .

America . . . is styled commonly the new world in respect of what was known in *Ptolemies* time. And this name imports glory enough, that she singly can equalize the title of World . . .

. . . And since she hath enough upon due right to prefer her worth, there will be no need of that counterfeit gloze of ancientry, which many pretend in the search of her originall . . . In brief, my line will reach . . . to the time of *Christopher Columbus* . . . They are no petty theeves that would steal from one his immortality: as what lesse could he deserve, that gave us the knowledge of another world, and laid the way open for the entrance of the Gospel, to the saving (as we hope) many millions of souls?

. . . His lights were little besides his own projecting wit, excellent skill in Astronomy and Navigation: by which he fully perswades himself of some lands, that must needs lie in that portion of circle, which should make up the world into a Globe, and withall saw, there could be no distemper either of heat or cold, that could make it lesse habitable or fruitfull, then [*recte* than] those places of the old world, which lay under the same Climates, and had the like respect to the heavens. These indeed were good rationall perswasions, but the difficulty would have daunted a mean spirit, and dasht not the action onely, but the very thought . . .

. . . When the gap was once opened many rushed in, and in a short space discovered a large Territory. *Americus Vesputius* got ground up on the Continent, and gave it that name . . .

. . . by reason of her length and breadth, she lyeth at such severall distance in respect of the heavens, that she admits indeed all variety almost, either of plenty or want, which we have hitherto found in *Asia*, *Africa*, or *Europe*. Here admirable for the fertility of soyl; then again as barren: here temperate, there scorching hot, elsewhere as extream cold. Some Regions watered with dainty Rivers, others again infested with perpetuall drouth. Some Plaines, some Hils, some Woods, some Mines, and what not in some tract or other within the compasse of *America*? yet nothing almost common to the whole but Barbarisme of manners, Idolatry in Religion, and sottish ignorance, such as hardly distinguisheth them from brutes: else they would not have taken reasonable men to be immortall Gods, as at first they did: yet what either God was, or immortality, they knew no more then [*recte* than] instinct of nature gave them, onely a confused thought they had of some place or other (God knows where) behinde some Hill . . .

Map of America, 1646
Published in *A Prospect of the Most Famous Parts of the World*
California is shown as a separate island

. . . their Customes are answerable to their Religion, beastly. They goe naked, and are very lustfull people without distinction of sexe . . . They labour not much to sustain themselves: but are rather content to take what the earth can yeeld without Tillage. This is generall . . .

Virginia carries in her name the happy memory of our Elizabeth. On the East it hath *Mare del Nort*, on the North *Norumbega*, *Florida* on the South, and West-ward, the bounds are not yet set. It was first entred by Sir *Walter Raleigh*, 1584, and some at that time left there to discover the Country till more were sent, but they perished before the second supply. Since, there have been many Colonies planted out of *England*, which have there manured the ground, and returned good Commodities to the Adventurers. For indeed it is a rich Country, in Fruit, Trees, Beasts, Fish, Fowle, Mines of Iron and Copper, Veins of Pitch, Allum, and Tarre, Rozen, Gummes, Dies, Timber, &c. The Plantation went on with good successe till the year 1622. And then by the treachery of the Inhabitants there were murdered neer upon three hundred of our men.[1] The Natives are very vile people, horrible Idolaters, adore the creature which they most fear, and hate them which keep them not in awe: they were kindly intreated by our *English*, and invited by all friendly means to Christianity. The North parts are most inhabited by our men, and is therefore called *New England* . . .'

A Prospect of the Most Famous Parts of the World (1646), pp. 9, 45–55.

[1] The massacre of 1622 took the almost defenceless colony by surprise and threatened the very existence of Virginia.

Colonial Troubles

English colonial life was firmly established by the mid-17th century. New colonies such as Maryland, North and South Carolina, New York and New Jersey were being added, trade and commerce were flourishing and the frontiers were beginning their westward expansion. In the first fifty years of the 18th century the population almost quadrupled to something like one and a half millions and the land area taken over was almost trebled.

The consolidation and expansion of British interests inevitably came into conflict with the equally ambitious, but eventually less successful, Spanish and French, also seeking supremacy in the New World. Decades of fighting were ushered in, culminating in the Treaty of Paris of 1763 by which British claims to North America were confirmed: westwards to the Mississippi, northwards to Canada, and southwards to Florida. Throughout the wars—and after—there was the continuing problem of the native Indians.

During these long years of conflict the British position was also seriously hampered by the lack of unity and co-operation both between, and within, the separate colonies.

'The principal officials in the colonies who were expected to enforce English laws and regulations were the royal and proprietary governors[1] . . . who suffered from responsibility without power. All except the governors of Virginia and of certain West Indian islands were dependent on the assemblies for their salaries . . . In the proprietary as in the royal governments, the assemblies, representing local interests, demanded greater control of their local affairs than the governors' instructions permitted; the governors demanded more power for their royal and proprietary masters than the people were disposed to admit; and distance, as well as the power of the purse, tended to keep the governor's power at a low ebb.'[2] The difficulty of fighting the enemy without, and dealing with squabbles within, is well illustrated by the problems faced by the proprietary governor of Pennsylvania, whose letters are quoted below.

One of the major problems faced by the British government and the individual governors in each colony was the difficulty of raising support for war supplies for a common and a united effort. 'Even in time of war, each colonial assembly had the privilege of honoring or dishonoring the requisitions made upon it by the home government for men, money and supplies. War grants generally had a number of strings attached which prevented the governor from employing colonial troops to best advantage, and often the grants were forthcoming only after concessions had been made on some issue over which governor and assembly had long been quarreling.'[3] Extracts of letters from the governors of Maryland and New York are also reproduced here, underlining the individual temper of some of the colonies even when facing the common enemy.

---

[1] Some of the colonies, such as Maryland and Pennsylvania, were granted to individual proprietors. The proprietors, working through resident governors, were thus able to establish their own vast private domains.

[2] Morison & Commager, vol. 1, *op. cit.*, pp. 94–95.

[3] Morison & Commager, vol. 1, *op. cit.*, p. 95.

GLOOM FROM THE GOVERNOR OF PENNSYLVANIA

A series of three 18th century copies of letters from William Denny, Governor of Pennsylvania, to Thomas Penn, mainly about the defence of the colonies against the French and the Indians. Thomas Penn, son of William Penn,[1] the founder of Pennsylvania, exercised proprietary jurisdiction over the colony. Returning to England in 1741 he managed his proprietary rights solely by correspondence.[2] In these three letters to Penn in England, Denny emphasises the problems he faced not only from the enemy, but also in working with the Provincial Commissioners and the Quakers.

i   Frontier attacks by the French and Indians and troubles with the Provincial Commissioners: letter from Philadelphia, 8 November 1757.

'. . . The Provincial Commissioners have been advised to advance proper Sums for Intelligence, and other necessary Services, and . . . it was recommended to them to put the Money into the Hands of the Field Officers . . . to be disposed . . . as occasions should present; but this was obstinately objected to by the Commissioners, who alledged this would be to give the disposition of the publick Money out of their Hands, which they could not consent to: so that I am under great disadvantages as to the knowledge of the Strength and motion of the Enemy. I am, however, well assured . . . of the truth of the following particulars: . . . That the French had not during the last Summer more than three hundred and fifty Men in Garrison at Fort Duquesne, till a reinforcement of Two hundred more . . . arrived there from the Mississippi, in twelve large Batteaus. That they have no Provisions from that River, but they are all sent from Canada . . . That the parties who now make the Incursions consist of Indians living on the North side of Lake Erie . . . and that these parties are fitted out [by the French] either at Fort Niagara, or their other Forts on the Ohio . . . who send with them, one or more Officers or Cadets with a small Detachment, as well to enure them to hardships and the Indian manner of Fighting, as to give them Opportunities of viewing what is doing on our Fronteers. That these Parties consist of Fifty or Sixty, or perhaps a greater Number when they arrive on the Fronteers; but if they find by their Advanced Scouts, that the Inhabitants are defenceless, they then divide into smaller Parties in order to do greater Mischief, burning Houses, killing Old People and such as make resistance, carrying off Children, and loading Horses, of which they are sure to find some at every Plantation, with the best of the Peoples' effects . . .

. . . the West part of the Province has been protected and the Harvest well got in, except some few of the Reapers, by their own Negligence and folly in not complying with their Orders, and refusing . . . to be guarded by Parties of Soldiers, were cut off by the Enemy Indians . . .

I have had great difficulties to recruit the Provincial Troops on Account of the Commissioners not allowing Proper Levy Money . . .

The Commissioners neglected all Summer my Advice, tho' repeatedly given them, to build Barracks [at Philadelphia]. After the return of Lord Loudoun with Troops, they began to think seriously about it, and in September assigned an order for eight Thousand pounds for

---

[1] For further references to William Penn see pp. 13, 98, 103, 104.
[2] *The Encyclopedia Americana*, vol. 21 (1968), p. 512.

that use . . . but without consulting me, they fixed on a . . . place between Schuylkill and the built part of the City, and expended a considerable Sum of Money in digging the foundation, tho' the Ground belonged to the Proprietaries, and no Application was made to their Agents . . . but all of a sudden they changed their minds and removed the materials from off that Spot, to another situate out of the City bounds, at the North end near the road leading from New York. The Ground was private property, and all the Lots near it, are so likewise . . . Work begun a second Time without my ever being consulted . . . I sent for the Plan and desired them not to go on till it was considered . . . They took no notice of my Letter, and in Contradiction to it carried on the building as expeditiously as they could . . .'

Goodwood MS. 183. no. 1 (a).

ii   Treaty-making with the Indians: letter from Philadelphia, 9 November 1757.

Denny complains that the Quakers 'were Officiously medling in matters of Government' in treating with the Indians. 'In this City [Philadelphia] as well as at Easton, they are even encouraging Teedyucung[1] and the other Indians to come to their Houses, entertaining them there . . . At Lancaster, they attended the Distribution of the Presents, and by their behaviour on that occasion plainly gave the Indians to understand, that they woud receive greater or lesser Presents, according to the Light in which the Quakers saw their Proceedings'.

There was the added problem that four of the Provincial Commissioners had acted without authority 'in providing the Presents to be made to the Indians . . . This is notorious and a flagrant breach of their Duty'. He objects to the 'exorbitant Quantity of Land' and the terms on which it was being offered to the Indians for 'their residence and hunting' and concludes with the difficulties of treaty-making[2] with Teedyuscung who 'hinted, as if he would go to England, if I did not do him justice here'. Teedyuscung's reluctance to co-operate is illustrated by the case of the carrying off of a woman and three of her children by an Indian scalping party.

Goodwood MS. 183, no. 1 (b).

iii   Denny relates his irritation with the Provincial Assembly over the raising of troops against the French and the terms of the Militia Bill and the Indian Trade Bill: letter from Philadelphia, 10 November 1757.

Express news had been sent by the Council of New York that 'Fort William Henry was invested by an Army of Eleven thousand French, Canadians, and Regulars'. The Assembly would take no immediate action and 'all I could do was to order a Return of the Powder in the Magazines and to lay an Embargo on it, and to apply to the Provincial Commissioners to enable me to raise such a Number of Men for the assistance of the Province of New York, as might be equal to their pressing necessities, and worthy of this Government'. The troops that were eventually raised were inadequately disciplined and many

---

[1]   Chief Teedyuscung of the Delaware Indians.
[2]   Between 1756 and 1758 a series of peace conferences was held to conclude agreements, known as the Treaty of Easton, between Pennsylvania, led by Governor Denny, and the Delaware Indians.

'Officers chosen by the People' had to be removed. A number of 'Substantial Citizens' of Philadelphia promised to march and recruit volunteers but no support materialised.

With the Militia Bill 'these infatuated People will rather fall a Sacrifice [to] the Enemy, than consent to a Law, which does not give them the choice of Officers, nor will the Quakers suffer a Bill which will effect them or hurt their Interest, and this present Bill is calculated to make one half of the People Quakers; it exempts all those, not who scrupulously and conscientiously are against bearing Arms, but who belong to the Congregations professing this Conscientious Scruple, by which means not only Quakers, but many other large Congregations of Germans, as well as all idle and cowardly People, who will for the sake of Exemption, very readily join themselves to, and frequent these Societies, will be exempted by Law from Personal Service and from providing Arms'.

The Indian Trade Bill is so framed 'in the oddest manner, that can be conceived. The Bill empowers the Provincial Commissioners to do all Acts relating to Government, as well as Commerce, such as distributing Presents to the Indians . . . the Bill enacts them to be done, not by me with the Approbation of the Commissioners: but by the Commissioners with my Approbation; such a Perversion of order, and such an insult on Government one would think impossible under an English Constitution'.

Denny concludes with information about a trading post for Indians at Fort Augusta and the building of 'a small Fort and some Log-houses' for the Indians at Wioming; the failure to repair the highways, and the passing of legislation including 'A Supply Act granting Four thousand Pounds to his Majesty's use . . . [partly] for the purchasing of cannon, small arms and ammunition'.

Goodwood MS. 183, no. 1 (c).

THE SPIRIT OF INDEPENDENCE

Jealous to preserve their independence and to determine their own affairs with minimal outside interference, the American colonies could show great reluctance to support the British government, even in times of war. These two letters from the governors of Maryland and New York were sent to Sir Charles Wyndham, 2nd Earl of Egremont, Secretary of State for the Southern Department. Egremont lived at Petworth House in Sussex and these communications are preserved in his letter book referring to military affairs in North America between December 1761 and August 1762.

i   Letter from Horatio Sharpe, Governor of Maryland, to Lord Egremont, 25 April 1762.

'It is not without great concern that I now write to your Lordship, that altho' I have in obedience to His Majesty's Commands . . . used my utmost endeavours to prevail on the General Assembly of this Province to levy Cloath and pay a Number of Troops for the King's Service, and to raise the Recruits which were demanded by Sir Jeffrey Amherst[1] as our Quota for the King's Regular Regiments on this Continent, my Endeavors have proved unsuccessfull . . .

---

[1] Governor-General of British North America, 1761–1763.

I pressed them to a Compliance with His Majesty's Requisition and
. . . for . . . Cloathing and paying, during the Term of one year, 400
Provincials and for raising 84 Recruits for the King's Regular Regiments . . . But . . . it was resolved by a Majority in . . . [the Lower]
House, that in Order to raise the Money . . . a Bill should be brought
in, as had eight Times before been rejected by the Upper House,
because in their Opinion it was calculated to introduce such Innovations in our constitution as would Create the greatest Confusion and
disorder, sacrifice a part of the Inhabitants to the Humour of the Rest,
and Invest the lower House of Assembly with executive Powers which
have hitherto been exercised by other Branches of our Legislature . . .
After the Upper House had returned with a Negative . . . a Motion was
made in the lower House for . . . a Sum of Money which is already in
our Treasury, but the same Majority . . . vehemently opposed this
Motion, nor would they even consent to the Appropriation of a Small
Sum Towards raising Recruits for the Regulars . . .

Being convinced by . . . their Conduct that it would Answer no good
End to keep them any longer Sitting, I yesterday, in compliance with
their request, put an End to the Session, and informed His Majesty's
General on this Continent of my having failed in my Endeavors to
procure him Assistance from this Province, and indeed I am afraid no
further Assistance will be given by our Assembly to His Majesty's
General during this War, if it is left to their Opinion, either to contribute or not . . .'

Petworth House Archives.

ii   Letter from Cadwallader Colden, Lieutenant-Governor of New York,
to Lord Egremont, 11 May 1762.

'. . . As the Number of Men inlisted in the beginning of this Month
came far Short of the Number required, I called the Assembly to meet
. . . and . . . I earnestly pressed them to give further encouragement to
Volunteers to inlist, and to compel Idle Persons into the King's Service,
who have no visible Way of living, and are Injurious to the community,
of which, I am informed, great numbers are in this Place at this Time,
but without Success . . .

. . . Nothing in my Power has been wanting to have compleated the
Numbers before this time . . . I shall continue my utmost Endeavours
for His Majesty's Service, tho' I am afraid it will be without Success in
Recruiting the Regulars, because I find an Aversion in the Assembly to
that part of the Service . . .'

Petworth House Archives.

TREATING WITH THE INDIANS

British colonial expansion in North America brought the new settlers and
traders into a direct confrontation with the native Indians. As their homelands and hunting grounds were overrun by the advancing frontiers, so
the British government urged tact and diplomacy in treating with the
Indians.

i   Writing to Sir Jeffrey Amherst, Governor-General of British North
America, Secretary of State Lord Egremont urged humanity and
indulgence in his letter from Whitehall, London, 12 December 1761.

'. . . It is needless to observe to you how much His Majesty's Interests
may be promoted by treating the Indians upon the . . . Principles of
Humanity and proper Indulgence. Your Knowledge of the Genius and
Turn of that People will suggest to you the more particular Rules for
your Conduct towards Them, which are left to your own Prudence.
I cannot, however, help mentioning to you one Circumstance . . .
which is so generally affirmed and credited, that I fear there must be
too much Foundation for it. It is said that the Indians are often disgusted and their Minds alienated from His Majesty's Government by
the shamefull Manner in which Business is Transacted between Them
and our Traders, the latter making no scruple of using every low Trick
and Artifice to over reach and Cheat those unguarded Ignorant
People in their Dealings with Them, while the French, by a different
Conduct, and worthy of our Imitation, deservedly gain their Confidence. It is superfluous to animadvert upon what so evidently obstructs
The King's Service, and dishonors the English Trader. It will naturally
excite your Indignation and call for what Redress may be in your
Power . . .'

Petworth House Archives.

Between 1759 and 1761 the Cherokee Indians took to the warpath in
their struggle for national survival. With their defeat in 1761, the
Cherokee leader Skiagusta Ocenesta, *alias* Osteneco, *alias* Judd's
Friend, Second Warrior of the Overhills, was invited to London to
meet King George III to seal the ties of friendship.[1]

ii   Letter to Secretary of State Lord Egremont from Francis Fauquier,
Lieutenant-Governor of Virginia, Williamsburg, 1 May 1762.

'. . . I have troubled Your Lordship and the rest of His Majesty's
Ministers with some very troublesome Guests who are a Cherokee
Chief named Skiagusta Oconesta, known also by the name of Judd's
Friend, and two of his Followers. These Indians have lately been
wavering between the French Interest and ours, and have lately con-
cluded a Peace with the King's Subjects at Charles Town, and have
given all possible demonstrations, in the Power of Man to give, of their
present good Intentions to us. Upon the pressing Instances of this
Man, the Council, seeing the great use it might be to His Majesty's
Service, that the Cherokees should be convinced of the Strength of the
British Nation, advised me to comply with His request, and this has
made me give Your Lordship the trouble of such Visitors.

Their being shewn the Grandeur of our Court, the great Warlike
Stores, the number of our Shipping able to Transport Warriors all over
the World, and the Infinite Number of our People compared to their

---

[1] David H. Corkran, *The Cherokee Frontier: Conflict and Survival, 1740–62* (1962), p. 266.
Facing p. 195 is an engraving of Osteneco on his visit to London in 1762, reproduced
from the *Royal Magazine of London* (July 1762). The engraving refers to him by yet
another name, Austenaco. The visits of North American Indians to England always
caused great excitement and formidable problems in spelling their names. In 1719
two American Indians came to London, creating sufficient interest for the parish clerk
of West Chiltington in Sussex to record in his parish register their seeing 'the Taming
of ye Shrew . . . at the Playhouse in Lundn'. His attempt at their names reads: 'The 1st
is son of the Emperor of the Nawcheys his name is Oakecharinga Tiggwawtubby
Tocholochy Yuca. The other is the son of the King Istowlawleys they call Tuskeestannagee Whosly Powon Micco.' (West Chiltington parish records, Par. 48/1/1/1.)

Small Towns, must give them great Ideas of the British Power and Wealth, and be attended with the best consequences to His Majesty's Subjects in this and the Neighbouring Colonies. And as the expense to the Crown will be very trifling in supporting them in their Way, I hope I shall not incur His Majesty's displeasure in what I have done, having Acted the best for his Service . . .'

Petworth House Archives.

iii Letter to Francis Fauquier from Lord Egremont, Whitehall, 10 July 1762.

'. . . Capt. Blake . . . also presented to me the Three Cherokees. You rightly observe that Such Visitors are always troublesome, and these Chiefs are become the more so from the Death of their Interpreter during the Voyage, which loss we have not been able to Supply. They are treated with all possible Civility and Attention, and it is hoped they will return to their own Country fully confirmed in all their good Intentions . . .'

Petworth House Archives.

iv 'Three *Cherokee Indian* chiefs arrived in *London* . . . They are well made men, near six feet high, were dressed in their own country habit, with only a shirt, trowsers, and mantle round them; their faces are painted of a copper colour, and their heads adorned with shells, feathers, ear-rings, and other trifling ornaments. They neither of them can speak to be understood, and very unfortunately lost their interpreter in their passage. A house is taken for them in *Suffolk street*, and cloaths have been given them in the *English* fashion.'

The Gentleman's Magazine, June 1762, p. 293.

v 'The *Cherokee* chiefs set out for *Portsmouth* on their return for *America*. In their way thither they visited *Winchester* camp, and dined with Lord *Bruce*. The next day they were conducted to the *French* prison, which they viewed with uncommon curiosity, expressing in the strongest terms their detestation of a people, from whom they had received so many instances of the most perfidious and cruel usage. In the afternoon they were shewn the college, and were entertained with fruit and wine by the Warden. The next morning the *Wiltshire* militia diverted them with an infinite variety of firings and evolutions for near two hours, which they beheld with remarkable attention and satisfaction. They then proceeded with Mr. *Montagu* and their interpreter[1] to *Portsmouth*, and saw the fortifications, ships, and dock-yard there, which struck them with such astonishment as they could not find words to express. Their general observation on being shewn these great objects is: That their *English* brethren can do everything . . .they went on board the *Epreuve* frigate (the same they came over in) and the wind being fair, sailed immediately.'

The Gentleman's Magazine, August 1762, p. 388.

---

[1] This reference to their now having an interpreter is almost certainly incorrect in view of Lord Egremont's concern about the whole matter expressed in his letter to the Governor of South Carolina (given in the next extract, no. vi).

vi Letter to Thomas Boone, Governor of South Carolina, from Lord
Egremont, Whitehall, London, 7 August 1762.

'This Letter will be delivered to You by Captain Blake, Commander
of One of His Majesty's Ships of War, appointed to carry back three
Cherokee Chiefs, who came here from Virginia . . . with an Interpreter
. . . but the Interpreter unfortunately died in the Voyage, and we have
not been able to find any person here who understands their Language,
which has put us under very great Difficulties to know their Wants.
However, every possible Attention has been paid to them, and I have
the Pleasure to inform You that they seem to leave this Country in
perfect good Temper, and greatly satisfied with the Presents that have
been made them.

The Services on which Capt. Blake's Ship is to proceed, make it necessary for him to land these Cherokees in Your Province, and I am to
signify to You the King's Pleasure that You do accordingly receive
them, and cause them to be conducted in the usual Manner into their
own Country. And as you doubtless have Persons in South Carolina
who Understand their Language, You will direct proper Compliments
to be made to them, in the King's Name, and express to them His
Majesty's Concern at the loss of their Interpreter, which must have
Subjected them to many Inconveniences during their Stay in England,
and you will assure them that it was the King's particular Order that
the utmost Attention should be paid to them. And in case that You
shall perceive they have been offended or disgusted with anything
that may have happened, You will endeavor to remove any ill Impressions they may have conceived by availing Yourself of the Circumstance
of the death of their Interpreter, and our not being able to understand
what they might wish to have, which you will assure them would have
been in every Respect complied with as far as Possible . . .'

Petworth House Archives.

SAVING COLONIAL SOULS

By the end of the 17th century the religious fervour that had originally
driven thousands of English and other Europeans to settle in the New
World was in danger of being lost. Many of the Puritan clergy feared the
worst. The Reverend Increase Mather predicted that America would be
the site of hell at the Last Judgement, and the Quaker William Penn was
convinced that his 'Holy Experiment' in founding Pennsylvania had
failed.[1] Desperate to fill the needs of the colonists with its own brand of
religion, the Anglican church founded the Society for the Propagation of
the Gospel in Foreign Parts in 1701 as the means to 'preserve and support,
in parts where it is so much wanted, true and genuine Christianity' in
the Plantations of America.[2] The religious zeal that followed the evangel-
ical revival in America—the Great Awakening started by the Reverend
George Whitefield in 1739—led to the founding of six colleges for young
people between 1746 and 1769.

---

[1] John C. Miller, *The First Frontier: Life in Colonial America* (1966), pp. 268–269.
[2] Anniversary sermon preached before the Society by the Bishop of Chichester, 15
February 1760, p. 12. Copy in West Sussex Record Office Library (Fuller Collection).

i   Proceedings of the Society for the Propagation of the Gospel in Foreign Parts from February 1759 to February 1760.

This annual report records the missionary work of the Society at the following stations: Newfoundland, Nova Scotia, New England, New York, New Jersey, Pennsylvania, North and South Carolina, Georgia and Barbados. Details include the appointment of clergy, the building of churches and schools, the baptism of whites, negroes and Indians, relationships with the dissenters and Anabaptists, and missionary work among British troops. Some of the problems in establishing church life are outlined. In New England the people of Frankfort pleaded for a minister although 'they are indeed very poor, being upon a Frontier Settlement, which they have been hitherto prevented from cultivating to Advantage, as it is exposed to the Insults of a barbarous Enemy; but they promise to contribute towards the Support of such Minister as much as they can . . . as soon as they enjoy the Blessing of Peace, they will build a Church, and a Parsonage House, and in the mean Time they can have *Richmond* Fort for an House for the Minister'. In the back part of South Carolina many of the people were 'sunk into a State of the grossest Ignorance for want of a settled Minister among them'.

West Sussex Record Office Library (Fuller Collection).

ii   Leaflet appealing for funds to support the Colleges of Philadelphia and New York, dated 9 September 1762. The particular leaflet referred to was received by the minister and churchwardens of the parish of Lyminster. The parish contributed £2. 7s. od. (£2.35) towards the appeal.

'At a Time when this happy Nation is exulting in a Series of the most important Successes, and hath given Protection and even Increase to her Dominions in the remotest Parts of the Earth; while *all* are ready to consider our distant Colonies and Acquisitions as an inexhaustible Source of future Wealth and Grandeur to the Public . . . there is one View more important still, in which we know you will delight to consider them . . . as promising to become an immense Addition to the KINGDOM OF CHRIST, and to the PROTESTANT CHURCH . . .

It would be needless to enumerate to you the lamentable Consequences of leaving a vast and increasing Multitude of our Fellow Subjects, in a remote Corner of the Earth, a Prey to Ignorance, open to the Corruptions of a vigilant Enemy, and continually exposed to *false* Notions of Religion and Government . . . LIBERTY does not deign to dwell but where her fair Companion KNOWLEDGE is; nor can Government be administered, but where the Principles of Justice, Virtue, Sobriety, and Obedience . . . are upheld.

It is of the utmost Consequence, therefore, to this Nation, that our Colonies should be made an Object of civil and religious Culture; and that all necessary Knowledge should not only be propagated among our own People there, but also among the Heathen around them, in order to root out their Notions of Barbarity, Murder, Rapine, Cruelty and Revenge, which are so fatal to us on every Difference with them. Without due Care in this respect, these immense Countries can never be rendered of full Use to these Kingdoms. Their Advantages of Soil, Climate and Situation, would not be improved for the Extension of our Commerce. They would be in Danger of becoming not only a very unprofitable, but even an unwieldy and dishonourable Appendage of this Monarchy; and, in the End, be so far from enlarging the *Church of Christ* and giving fresh Strength to the *Protestant Interest,* as to fall, perhaps, into the opposite Scale of Superstitition and Idolatry.

. . . no Institutions can be better calculated to answer these good Purposes . . . than [these] Colleges.

Near *Four Hundred Youths* are continually educated in them; of whom about Sixty are intended for the learned Professions, and particularly to furnish a Supply of Ministers and Teachers for the different Societies of Christians in these Parts. The Remainder are chiefly designed for Merchandize, Trade, Navigation, and the mechanic Professions . . .

But a great Check has been given to these undertakings by the Ravages of a destructive War,[1] which laid waste a considerable Part of both Provinces, increased the Expense of these Institutions . . . and forbid them to expect any speedy Assistance from their own Legislatures, on account of the vast Load of Public Debt accumulated for the Defence of the Country. They have, therefore, been severally obliged to have Recourse to the known Benevolence and Charity of the Friends of Religion and Learning in these Kingdoms . . .'

Par. 131/7/2.

'NO PROSPECTS BUT DESPAIR': THE GATHERING STORM

The notion that the colonies existed solely for the economic well-being of the mother country laid the ground for the mounting friction between the British government and the American colonists. The issue is discussed in the important document which follows,[2] written in 1765 by an un-identified New York merchant 'resident and concerned in Trade there upwards of Twenty Years'.

The writer outlines at some length the problems resulting from British insistence that the American colonists trade solely with Britain, a policy he foresees as leading to disastrous consequences, and which indeed just ten years later became a major cause of the outbreak of the revolutionary war.

i 'The Distressed and declining State of the British Empire in America from the Rigorous Execution of the Statutes . . . is become an Object of such universal Concern to the Mother Country & its Colonies, as to justify everybody in the least conversant with their Commercial Interest in an Attempt to point out the dangerous Consequences which these Statutes must inevitably produce . . .'

A list of the American colonies then follows: Canada, Nova Scotia, New Hampshire, Massachusetts Bay, Rhode Island and Providence Plantations, Connecticut, New Jersey, Pennsylvania, Maryland, Virginia, North and South Carolina, Georgia, East and West Florida and New York. In each case the produce of the colonies is given except

---

[1] The French and Indian Wars which were concluded by the Treaty of Paris in February 1763.

[2] This document came into the keeping of Charles, 3rd Duke of Richmond (1734/5–1806)—of Goodwood. The Duke urged the recognition of American independence. See Alison Olson, *The Radical Duke: The Career and Correspondence of Charles Lennox, Third Duke of Richmond* (1961), p. 37. He is reported as having flown the American colours on his yacht during the War of Independence: Philip Whitwell Wilson (ed.), *The Greville Diary,* vol. 2 (1927), p. 538. The other Goodwood documents referred to were also collected together by the 3rd Duke.

15

for the Floridas which are 'as yet so very inconsiderable in their Exports
& Imports'.

The trade in molasses is then considered as an example of the sufferings
being caused, the colonies now no longer being allowed to import from
'the foreign Islands'. Molasses were used by the poor as a substitute for
sugar, but more important, were used for making rum used in 'bartering
for Fish, and in trafficking with the Indians for Furs and Skins . . . In
the Indian Trade particularly, Rum is an Article so very essential, that
the Savages will scarcely deal without it: Besides this, the Article of
Rum, 'til the late Restrictions, made up a principal Part of the Cargoes
which the American Merchants employed in the Guinea Trade, and
brought them home Slaves, Beeswax, Gold & Ivory, which they sold to
a prodigious Advantage, and from which they gained new Resources
of discharging the astonishing Sums in which they stood indebted to
the Merchants of England. These Resources being cut off, as well as
their Fisheries, & their Indian Trade, they are left with no Prospects
but Despair . . .'

There then follows a detailed and closely argued case against the
restrictions imposed on American trade. Not only were the colonies
being damaged, for the harm would inevitably wound 'the Landed
Interest' in the mother country. 'The Rents of Houses must naturally
remain unpaid, the Value of Iron Works & Collieries must naturally
lessen, & in short the Connections of Trade being universal, the
Injuries which it suffers cannot but be universal too . . .'

Goodwood MS. 183, no. 4.

The War of Independence

Taxed, restricted and regulated beyond endurance by the British government, the American colonists petitioned and pleaded with George III's ministers and agents. Their failure to win concessions, and the increasing presence of British troops, clearly seemed to underline that resort to arms was inevitable. A few of the immediate preliminaries and early incidents of the War are here outlined from documents, journals and newspapers in the West Sussex Record Office.

i Petition to King George III from the American General Congress in Philadelphia, 26 October 1774.

'A standing army has been kept in these Colonies ever since the conclusion of the late war, without the consent of our Assemblies; and this army, with a considerable naval armament, has been employed to enforce the collection of taxes.

The authority of the Commander in Chief, and under him, of the Brigadiers General, has, in time of peace, been rendered supreme in all the civil governments in America.

The Commander in Chief of all your Majesty's forces in North-America has, in time of peace, been appointed Governor of a Colony . . .

The officers of the customs are empowered to break open and enter houses without the authority of any civil magistrate . . .

Humble and reasonable petitions from the Representatives of the People have been fruitless . . .

Assemblies have been repeatedly and injuriously dissolved.

Commerce has been burthened with many useless and oppressive restrictions . . .

In the last sessions of Parliament, an act was passed for blocking up the harbour of Boston; another, empowering the Governor of the Massachussetts-Bay to send persons indicted for murder in that province to another colony, or even to Great-Britain, for trial, whereby such offenders may escape legal punishment; a third, for altering the chartered constitution of government in that province; and a fourth, for extending the limits of Quebec, abolishing the English and restoring the French laws, whereby great numbers of British freemen are subjected to the latter, and establishing an absolute government, and the Roman Catholic religion . . . and a fifth, for the better providing suitable quarters for officers and soldiers in his Majesty's service in North-America.

To a Sovereign who "glories in the name of Briton", the bear recital of these acts must, we presume, justify the loyal subjects who fly to the foot of his throne, and implore his clemency for protection against them.

From this destructive system of Colony administration, adopted since the conclusion of the last war, have flowed those distresses, dangers, fears, and jealousies, that overwhelm your Majesty's dutiful Colonies with affliction . . .

Had our Creator been pleased to give us existence in a land of slavery, the sense of our condition might have been mitigated by ignorance and habit. But thanks be to his adorable goodness, we were born the heirs of freedom, and ever enjoyed our right under the auspices of your royal ancestors, whose family was seated on the British throne to rescue and secure a pious and gallant nation from the popery and despotism of a superstitious and inexorable tyrant. Your Majesty, we are confident . . . that your title to the crown is thus founded on the title of your people to liberty . . .

We ask but for peace, liberty, and safety. We wish not a diminution of the prerogative, nor do we solicit the grant of any new right in our favour. Your royal authority over us, and our connection with Great Britain, we shall always carefully and zealously endeavour to support and maintain.

. . . we solemnly profess, that our councils have been influenced by no other motive, than a dread of impending destruction . . .

We therefore most earnestly beseech your Majesty, that your royal authority and interposition may be used for our relief . . .'
The Gentleman's Magazine, January 1775, pp. 20–23.

ii   The House of Lords resolves that the Common Hangman in London be ordered to burn a 'false, malicious, and dangerous' pamphlet, 24 February 1775.

'Lord Effingham complained of the licentiousness of the press, and produced a pamphlet, entituled, The Present Crisis with respect to America considered, published by T. Becket, which his Lordship declared to be a most daring insult on the King, and moved, that the House would come to resolutions to the following effect:

That the said pamphlet is a false, malicious, and dangerous libel, subversive of the principles of the glorious revolution, to which we owe our present invaluable constitution, and of the rights of the people.

That one of the said pamphlets be burnt by the hands of the common hangman in Old Palace-yard, and another at the Royal Exchange.'
The Gentleman's Magazine, March 1775, pp. 146–147.

iii   As pamphlet warfare mounted on both sides of the Atlantic, news filtering through from America gave every sign that open hostilities on the battlefield were not far away. News published by *The Gentleman's Magazine* in April 1775 included the following reports:

'By accounts just received from America, there is advice, that General Gage, having information that some cannon were lodged in or near Salem, sent an officer to discover the place, and also ordered a detachment from the 64th regiment to bring them away; but the populace had been beforehand with them, and had carried them off before the soldiers arrived . . .

By a ship just arrived at Bristol from America, it is reported, that the Americans have hoisted their standard of liberty at Salem . . .

A ship arrived . . . from New York; but her letters have been kept back, and her dispatches kept secret. It is, however, transpired, that the provincials are regularly exercised every week, and that they seem determined to take the field, in case the prayer of the Continental Congress is disregarded . . .

In part of a letter from Boston . . . it is said, that Capt. Brown, and another

18

officer of the 52d regiment, at Boston, being sent to take a survey of the roads about that country, very narrowly escaped being tarred and feathered at Marlborough. They were entertained there by a Mr. Barnes, and, though in disguise, were discovered by a drummer, who had formerly deserted from the same regiment. The consequence was, the people assembled in great numbers, and surrounded the house; the two officers got to Boston, but Mr. Barnes's house was almost tore to pieces . . .

Letters of good authority from America affirm, that the militia of Massachussetts bay and Connecticut are actually embodied, have magazines ready prepared, and are assembled to the number of 12,000 effective men; that Salem was the head-quarters when the letters were written; but that a considerable body were on their march to Boston; so that there is not a doubt but that the next news will be an account of a bloody engagement between the two armies.'

The Gentleman's Magazine, April 1775, pp. 203–205.

iv   The First Shots: Lexington and Concord, 19 April 1775.

The Governor of Massachusetts, General Gage, ordered the Boston garrison to destroy the arms supply being built up at Concord by the provincial militia. On the morning of 19 April 1775 their march to Concord was barred at Lexington. British and American troops faced each other across the green and the first shots were fired. The War was on. Nobody knows with certainty who fired first, both sides laying the charge on the other. To the American patriot it was a brutal and un-provoked attack. *The London Gazette* 'published by authority' a different story:

'Lieut. Col. Smith, finding, after he had advanced some miles on his march, that the country had been alarmed by the firing of guns and ringing of bells, dispatched six companies of light infantry, in order to secure two bridges on different roads beyond Concord, who, upon their arrival at Lexington, found a body of the country people drawn up under arms on a green close to the road; and upon the King's troops marching up to them, in order to enquire the reason of their being so assembled, they went off in great confusion, and several guns were fired upon the King's troops from behind a stone wall, and also from the meeting-house and other houses . . . In consequence of this attack by the rebels, the troops returned the fire, and killed several of them; after which the detachment marched on to Concord . . . where they effected the purpose for which they were sent, having knocked off the trunnions of three pieces of iron ordnance, burnt some new gun carriages, and a great number of carriage-wheels, and thrown into the river a considerable quantity of flour, gunpowder, musket-balls, and other articles . . .

On the return of the troops from Concord, they were very much annoyed, and had several men killed and wounded, by the rebels firing from behind walls, ditches, trees, and other ambushes . . . and such was the cruelty and barbarity of the rebels, that they scalped and cut off the ears of some of the wounded men, who fell into their hands.'

Reprinted in The Gentleman's Magazine, June 1775, p. 293.

v   The Battle of Bunker Hill, 17 June 1775.

Boston, as the British garrison town, gave the setting for the first major battle of the War of Independence. Just over the harbour, on the heights above Charlestown, American patriots dug themselves into a formidable strategic position from which they might have blasted the British out of Boston. General Gage decided on an offensive: a display of force by a frontal attack on Charlestown. Although the hill was eventually taken and the patriots forced to retreat it was something of a hollow victory as redcoat casualties were so great.

The engagement is recorded on a map, published in London in 1775, in the West Dean Archives, entitled 'A Sketch of the Action between the British Forces and the American Provincials on the Heights of the Peninsula of Charlestown, the 17th of June 1775', at a scale of $4\frac{1}{2}$ inches to 1 mile. The map shows the route of the British troops from Boston to their landing at Charlestown and the position of the Americans; the confrontation, and the American retreat through the Charlestown Neck to Cambridge.

West Dean MS. 3189.

vi Another map in the West Dean Archives is a plan of Boston and its immediate environs showing streets (unnamed), principal buildings (named), topographical features and military works constructed in 1775 and 1776. At a scale of $4\frac{1}{2}$ inches to 1 mile, this was published by Henry Pelham in London in 1777. For a further reference to this map see below, pp. 97–98.

West Dean MS. 3190.

vii The Plea for Neutrality.

This pamphlet, reprinted from the *White-Hall Evening Post* for 10 February 1776, urges neutrality by the United Provinces in the conflict between Britain and America. Recommending a refusal to King George III's request for the loan of troops, it was published with the intention of showing 'in how odious a light our unnatural civil war with America does appear to all the powers of Europe, and which by its fatal and inevitable consequences must ruin the trade and commerce of this once happy nation'.

'Assisting a foreign power with troops, in order to extricate them from troubles in which they are involved, is simply no less than engaging therein, chusing a party, and putting ourselves in danger of being deeper involved than may at first be foreseen or wished for, and thus exposing ourselves to all the consequences of the first step . . .

The torch which now burns in America, is capable of inflaming all Europe, already full of combustibles . . .

In what an odious light must this unnatural civil war appear to all Europe; a war in which even Savages (if credit can be given to Newspaper information) refuse to engage; more odious still would it appear for a people to take a part therein, who were themselves once slaves, bore that hateful name, but at last had spirit to fight themselves free: But above all, it must appear superlatively detestable to me, who think the Americans worthy every man's esteem, and look on them as a brave people defending in a becoming, manly, and religious manner, those rights, which as men they derive from God, not from the Legislature of Great Britain.'

Goodwood MS. 209.

viii   The Dean of Gloucester enters the Fray.

Josiah Tucker,[1] Dean of Gloucester, pamphleteer, economist and divine, became famous for his advocacy that the colonists be separated from the mother country. He held the view that the American trade was of little advantage to Britain and that the colonists should be excluded from participation in the benefits of Empire. In 1775 he argued his case in *An humble Address and earnest Appeal to those respectable Personages in Great Britain and Ireland, who, by their great and permanent Interest in landed Property, their liberal Education, and enlarged Views, are the ablest to judge, and the fittest to decide, whether a Connection with, or a Separation from, the Continental Colonies of America, be most for the national Advantage, and the lasting Benefit of these Kingdoms.*

Soon after publication the following lines by Soame Jenyns were inserted in *The Gentleman's Magazine*:

> 'CROWN'D be the man with lasting praise
>   Who first contriv'd the pin
> To loose mad horses from the chaise,
>   And save the necks within.
>
> See how they prance, and bound, and skip,
>   And all controul disdain!
> They bid defiance to the whip,
>   And tear the silken rein.
>
> Awhile we try if art or strength
>   Are able to prevail;
> But, hopeless, when we find at length
>   That all our efforts fail.
>
> With ready foot the spring we press,
>   Out jumps the magic plug,
> Then, disengag'd from all distress,
>   We sit quite safe and snug.
>
> The pamper'd steeds, their freedom gain'd,
>   Run off full speed together;
> But, having no plan ascertain'd,
>   They run they know not whither.
>
> Boys, who love mischief and a course,
>   Enjoying the disaster,
> Bawl, stop 'em! stop 'em! till they're hoarse,
>   But mean to drive them faster.
>
> Each, claiming now his nat'ral right,
>   Scorns to obey his brother;
> So they proceed to kick and bite,
>   And worry one another.
>
> Hungry at last, and blind, and lame,
>   Bleeding at nose and eyes,
> By suff'rings grown extremely tame,
>   And by experience wise.

---

[1]   1712–1799.

> With bellies full of liberty,
> But void of oats and hay,
> They both sneak back, their folly see,
> And run no more away.
>
> Let all who view th' instructive scene,
> And patronize the plan,
> Give thanks to Glo'ster's honest Dean,
> For, TUCKER, thou'rt the man!'

The Gentleman's Magazine, March 1776, p. 133.

ix 'We hold these truths to be self evident . . .': The Declaration of Independence, 1776.

The Declaration of Independence, adopted unanimously by the thirteen United States of America on 4 July 1776 announced the birth of the new nation.

In giving the formal catalogue of the political and economic grievances leading to the resolution by Congress 'that all political connection between them and the state of Great Britain is and ought to be totally dissolved' the fundamental precept of the revolution was declared: that 'all men are created equal . . . with certain unalienable rights . . . that to secure these rights, Governments are instituted . . . deriving their just powers from the consent of the Governed. That whenever any form of Government becomes destructive of these ends it is the right of the people to alter or to abolish it and to institute new Government . . .'

The original document signed at Philadelphia is now preserved in the National Archives, Washington, D.C. The manuscript of the Declaration in the West Sussex Record Office is an undated, but early, parchment copy.

Add. MS. 8981.

x The Long Island Campaign, 1776.

By early 1776 British strategy was centred on New York 'emotionally and geographically . . . the weakest link in the thirteen rebellious colonies'.[1] In the summer it was seized without difficulty and Washington was forced to retreat northwards to Harlem.

A further map in the West Dean Archives shows the northern part of 'New York Island' with a plan of Fort Washington ('now Fort Knyphausen', named after the Hessian commander, Lieutenant-General Knyphausen) and battery points, and 'the Rebel Lines to the Southward' which were attacked by a combined force of British and Hessian troops on 16 November 1776. The position of Harlem is also shown. This was published in London in 1777 at a scale of 3 inches to 1 mile.

West Dean MS. 3191.

xi The Press and the War, 1777.

American affairs reported in *The London Packet; or New Lloyd's Evening Post* for 3–5 December 1777.

In the House of Lords the Duke of Richmond[2] pressed for an immediate enquiry into the state of the nation's defences on account of the American

---

[1] R. B. Nye & J. E. Morpurgo, *A History of the United States: vol. 1, The Birth of the U.S.A.* (3rd edn. 1970), p. 221.
[2] See p. 15.

war (p. 1) as 'we were still as distant from the object of peace, as at the commencement of this ruinous war. What it had cost the nation in men and money. The losses which our commerce had sustained. And the defensive state of this country, were matters of such infinite consequence as to require parliamentary deliberation. It was necessary to be informed of the true state of the nation'. Lord Chatham[1] added his sympathy, expressing the view that the Americans were 'HONEST REBELS FIGHTING FOR LIBERTY . . . Generous treatment on our part would have induced an honourable confidence on the part of America . . . We had lost America. We had waged a civil war which might prove fatal to the empire. We had invaded America. We had laid waste the country of our friends . . .'

Two Commons debates are then reported (pp. 2, 3) the second mainly concerned with the news of General Burgoyne's surrender at Saratoga.[2] Edmund Burke[3] drew attention to American generosity after this surrender as 'Our army was totally at their mercy: We had engaged the Indians to butcher them, their wives and children; and yet, generous to the last degree, they give our men leave to depart on their parole, never more to bear arms against North America'.

A report of the surrender follows (pp. 3, 4). 'The purport of the terms of capitulation is, that the British army should march out of their camp, lay down their arms, become prisoners of war, engage not to serve during the war, shall go to Boston, and from thence to England. All the arms, colours, cannons, stores, &c. &c. together with the military chest, containing 70,000 guineas, are given up to the Americans. These conditions were agreed to. A victory, so complete, has not happened in the history of modern times.'

Goodwood MS. 211.

---

[1] William Pitt, the Elder (1708–1778).

[2] General Burgoyne's surrender at Saratoga, 17 October 1777, marked the failure of his northern campaign to take the Hudson Valley and thereby drive a wedge between New England and the middle and southern states. Burgoyne returned to England in disgrace. This was the turning point in the war as it stirred France to enter the war in support of the Americans.

[3] 1729–1797, statesman, writer, and at this time M.P. for Bristol. He advocated peace with America.

Aftermath of War: the Need for Unity

With the war won and independence for America at last ratified by the Treaty of Paris in 1783, the new nation had now to come to terms with its own internal organisation and government. National unity had to be forged, a heterogeneous people of widely differing backgrounds and local interests welded together into one nation.

i   George Washington, first President of the United States, worn out by the bitter struggles of political life, made a last desperate appeal for unity in his Farewell Address in 1796.

The Address was reported in *The Times* in two parts. The first part, parts of which are reproduced here, was reported in the edition of 9 November 1796.

'The unity of Government which constitutes you one people, is . . . dear to you . . . it is a main pillar in the edifice of your real independence, the support of your tranquillity at home, your peace abroad; of your safety; of your prosperity; of that very liberty which you so highly prize . . . much pains will be taken, many artifices employed, to weaken in your minds the conviction of this truth . . .

For this you have every inducement of sympathy and interest. Citizens by birth or choice, of a common country, that country has a right to concentrate your affections. The name of AMERICA, which belongs to you, in your national capacity, must always exalt the just pride of patriotism, more than any appellation deriving from local discrimin- ations. With slight shades of difference, you have the same religious manners, habits and political principles . . .

. . . every portion of your country finds the most commanding motives for carefully guarding and preserving the union of the whole.

The NORTH, in an unrestrained intercourse with the SOUTH . . . finds in the productions of the latter, great additional resources of maritime and commercial enterprise, and precious materials of manufacturing indus- try. The SOUTH, in the same intercourse, benefiting by the agency of the NORTH, sees its agriculture grow and its commerce expand . . . The EAST, in a like intercourse with the WEST . . . will more and more find a valuable vent for the commodities which it brings from abroad, or manufactures at home. The WEST derives from the EAST supplies requisite to its growth and comfort . . .

In contemplating the causes which may disturb our Union, it occurs as matter of very serious concern, that any ground should have been furnished for characterizing parties by GEOGRAPHICAL discriminations. . . . One of the expedients of party to acquire influence . . . is to mis- represent the opinions and aims of other districts . . .

Towards the preservation of your Government, and the permanency of your present happy State, it is requisite, not only that you steadily discountenance irregular oppositions to its acknowledged authority, but also that you resist with care the spirit of innovation upon its principles . . .

Let me now . . . warn you in the most solemn manner against the baneful effects of the spirit of party . . .

It serves always to distract the Public Councils and enfeeble the Public Administration. It agitates the Community with ill-founded jealousies and false alarms; kindles the animosity of one part against another, foments occasionally riot and insurrection. It opens the door to foreign influence and corruption . . .'

Hawkins Papers 26.

'Free Trade and Sailors' Rights': War with Britain Again

The economic warfare waged between Britain and Napoleon in the early 19th century tightened its grip on American commerce with Europe. British Orders in Council and French Decrees created a tangle of problems for American shipping, both belligerents seizing all ships found trading with the other side. Adding insult to injury, Britain insisted on the right to press-gang alleged naval deserters by searching American shipping. War fever raged in 1807 when the British frigate *Leopard* intercepted the U.S.S. *Chesapeake* for deserters. British guns were fired, American sailors killed and four alleged deserters removed. As provocation on the high seas mounted, the 'war hawks' in Congress clamoured for war against Britain, eager for the chance to drive the British from Canada and from their influence in encouraging Indian resistance to American expansion westwards. War was declared by Congress in June 1812.

During the war a major part of the British offensive was the blockade of the American seaboard from New England to Louisiana. America tottered to the brink of ruin as trade was brought to a virtual standstill. With Napoleon's surrender in April 1814, British troops and ships became available to intensify the American operation: the blockade was extended and invasions planned from Canada in the north, New Orleans in the south, and up the Chesapeake inlet on the east coast.

One ship to take part both in the blockade and the Chesapeake invasion was H.M.S. *Brune*, commanded by Captain William Stanhope Badcock, whose family papers are in the West Sussex Record Office.[1] Some of these papers relate to Badcock's distinguished naval career,[2] and in particular to the Chesapeake operation of 1814.

i   Log-book of H.M.S. *Brune* on its voyage from Portsmouth, 7 April 1814, to Bermuda, and thence to Chesapeake Bay, with 'A narrative of our proceedings in the River Patuxent from the 15th of July to the 5th September'. (The narrative in fact was discontinued on 22 August.)

Badcock's narrative describes the British operations in the Patuxent: blockading, foraging missions, military sorties and the escape of American-owned slaves to the British ships. On 20 August H.M.S. *Brune* took part in the landing of over four thousand British and German troops at Benedict. From here the troops went on to attack and destroy Washington, the new capital of the United States.

'On the 15th July we joined Adml. Cockburne whose flag was on board the *Albion* . . . at anchor at the entrance of the river Patuxent . . .

The morning of the 16th I received orders to put myself under the command of Captain Nourse of the *Severn*, for the purpose of assisting to blockade the enemy's Gun boats laying up the river, commanded by Commodore Barney, who had his broad pennant flying in a sloop of

---

[1] Add. MSS. 1344–1412.

[2] Prior to the American operation he had served in the royal navy in the Adriatic and Mediterranean during the Napoleonic Wars. He served on H.M.S. *Neptune* at Trafalgar. His own personal account of his naval career was published after he had changed his surname to Lovell. See Vice-Admiral William Stanhope Lovell, *Personal Narrative of Events, from 1799 to 1815* (2nd edn. 1879, reprinted 1971).

8 guns, and had under his command 17 gun boats, generally mounting a long 12, 18, or 24 pounder in the bow, and a 32 pound carronade astern, manned with from fifty to sixty men in each . . . we . . . got under sail with the intention of going up to the village of Benedict . . . 30 miles from the entrance. Owing to light winds we were prevented from getting nearer to it than five miles. We therefore at 8 anchored in 7 fathoms off Battle Creek. Admiral Cockburne with the other ships proceeded up the river Potomac to distress the enemy on that side, while we annoyed him and blockaded his Gun boats in this river, who, as we advanced, retired up the river to Nottingham, a small town 25 miles above Benedict. We could not follow them with the ships on account of the shoalness of the water.

Sunday the 17th at 2 in the morning the Boats of the Squadron, manned and armed, left the ship, taking with them three hundred Marines, and . . . landed at a point of land . . . called God's Grace, and marched to Hunting town, a small place seven miles off, destroyed a few Arms and burnt a Tobacco store with 150 hogsheads of Tobacco in it, and brought away 19 Hogsheads which we put into the Boats, and at three in the afternoon, embarked the Marines and Seamen, without loss, or accident, except that a few were attacked by a Coup de Soleil[1] but recovered. We saw nothing of the enemy, but heard that some of the Militia had retired into the woods four miles off, being (to use an American expression) 'quite scared'.

On the 18th we had heavy thunder, lightening and rain. 8 black men, 4 women and 3 children came . . . to us in a small canoe. The 19th we again landed and marched 7 miles through the woods to attack the Militia at Frederick town. On our arrival there, we found they had marched away. We therefore burnt the Court House and Jail, and marched back through the woods to our Boats, driving the Bullocks, Sheep & Pigs before us, and almost every man carrying a Goose, Turkey or Fowl.

On the 20th we landed on the opposite side of the river, burnt a Tobacco store and brought away eleven Hogsheads, some Cattle &c. &c. This day we saw a few of the enemy's Cavalry and Infantry, whom we fired at . . .

The 22d in the morning we shifted our Anchorage lower down the river, the Natives having driven their Stock into the woods, to prevent our marauding parties from getting it. We . . . landed with 300 Marines and marched nine miles into the country, partly through thick woods, which an enterprising enemy would have taken advantage of, and cut us all off. In this excursion we went to the Parson of the Parish, who had received into his Store for protection some property belonging to the Parishioners. We made him find Carts and Horses, and then loaded them with Tobacco &c. and escorted them down to the Boats . . .

On the 23d we weighed [anchor] and ran down to Sandy Point . . . and the 24th the boats were employed getting Wood from the shore under the protection of a guard of Marines and an 18 pounder carronade in the Launch.

---

[1] Badcock recorded the temperature for this day as 80°F.

The morning of the 25th one of my ships company deserted to the enemy . . . we . . . ran down to Drum Point, the entrance of the river, landed some Marines as a Guard and sent Boats to get water. At 4 came in a Tornado from the West . . . its force was so great that it upset . . . one of our schooner Gun boats . . . Its fury was spent in about ten minutes, but during its continuance it tore up large trees by the roots, and blew down a large barn. It may easily be guarded against by keeping a look out to the West (for it always comes from that quarter), and when you see a very black cloud accompanied with a clap of thunder and lightening and a very angry looking sky . . . have your . . . Anchors ready for letting go.

From the 26th to the 30th was taken up compleating our wood and water, which we did under the protection of a Guard of Marines. Our Main yard being sprung[1] & the ship wanting other spars, I sent a party of men into the woods [to] cut a spar for a Main yard, three top gallant masts, a mizen top sail yard, jib boom, and three stay sail masts . . .

On the 4th [August] . . . 28 blacks, men, women & children came . . . to us . . . On the 7th two black men, two women and five children came on board in a canoe, and on the 8th nine more. On the 9th punished three men for drunkeness . . .

On the 12th we sent 45 blacks to Tangier Island (a small, barren, sandy, swampy place that we took possession of) to wait for an opportunity of going to Halifax or Bermuda, and likewise to endeavour to get the men to enlist into the Black Colonial Marine corps, at present organising there. Guard boats went every night above Leonards Creek to row till daylight, to prevent the enemy from sending down fire vessels . . . The 16th . . . A black man who had come on board a few days ago, asked permission to be landed at night, that he might endeavor to get off his wife. The poor fellow never came back, and we have since heard he was hung.

On the 17th in the evening, the *Tonnant* . . . *Albion* . . . *Royal Ark* . . . several frigates and brigs with 20 sail of Transports with the 4th, 21st, 44th and 85th Regts. and the Marine battalion arrived off the mouth of the river. Major Genl. Ross commanded the Troops . . . On the morning of the 20th, we landed all the Troops, and at noon we anchored two miles from the town of Benedict.

On Saturday the 20th all the boats of the squadron, manned and armed, left the ships, and advanced up the river towards Lower Malbro', to attack the Gun Boats and likewise to act as the right flank of our army. The enemys flotilla retired 60 miles up the river to a place called Pig point.

Sunday the 21st the boats reached Nottingham late in the evening and our army arrived there a few minutes after. A few of the enemy's Cavalry galloped out of the town, and the boats fired upon them. At noon the 22d, our boats fell in with the enemy's Gun boats, who ran them on shore and blew them all up except one . . . [which we] brought away . . . One division of boats proceeded to Upper Malbro' to keep up communication with our Army, the remainder continued

---

[1] A nautical term meaning to be split or warped out of shape.

at Pig point all that night and the next, and loaded some schooners with Tobacco.'[1]

Add. MS. 1382.

ii Plan of part of the River Patuxent, printed by Charpentier, Portsmouth, England, 1814.

The plan, at a scale of 1 inch to 2 miles, shows the Patuxent from its estuary on the Chesapeake between Cedar Point and Drum Point and Upper and Lower Malborough. Gives depth of water, marker points and the route of the British march from Benedict towards Washington. H.M.S. *Severn* and H.M.S. *Brune* are shown in the lower reaches of the Patuxent. See plate no. II for part of this plan.

Add. MS. 1376.

iii Troop landings at Benedict, 20 August 1814.

Official order from Captain of the Fleet Edward Codrington, giving tabulated information about the use of craft for the landing of troops at the Chesapeake invasion. The order relates to three divisions, each listing the names of ships and a description of the landing craft, the number of men to be landed in each, their respective regiments and the name of the transports which had brought the troops from Europe.

There is also a plan of the disposition of the landing craft under the command of Captains Badcock, Dillon, and Lieutenant Jones-Strombolo, giving the number of troops to each boat and the names of their regiments. Troops of the German Legion are listed. Cutters and yawls were used to tow four launches carrying 'Field Pieces' and howitzers to the shore.

Add. MS. 1375.

iv The twist of fortune: the blockaders on short rations, November 1814.

The Chesapeake offensive was over in September 1814, with Washington burnt to the ground, but with a successful American defence of Baltimore and Fort McHenry.[2] British and German troops departed.

Captain Badcock in H.M.S. *Brune* was ordered to remain and continue the Chesapeake blockade.[3] As October wore on the British forage parties raiding the shore were having less and less success in finding provisions. By 1 November the following order was issued by Captain Robert Barrie, senior officer of the remaining squadron:

'The Provisions of the Squadron under my command getting extremely low, and it being very uncertain at this advanced season of the Year when a supply can arrive, I find myself under the painful necessity of placing the Ships' Companys and Troops at short allowance.

You are therefore to place the Crew and Troops on board the Ship you command at half allowance of Bread and so to proportion your other Provisions (substituting one Article of Provisions for another as in your

---

[1] At this point the narrative is discontinued. Badcock, however, went on with the troops and was at the capture of Washington two days later.

[2] It was during the bombardment of Fort McHenry that Francis Key Smith composed America's national anthem, the 'Star Spangled Banner'.

[3] During the continuing blockade, military sorties to the shore went on as before. In a memorial to the Admiralty (Add. MS. 1380), Badcock refers to the taking of the town of Rappahannock (in early November) where the American colours bearing the slogans 'Death or Victory' and 'Keep the Tyrants down' were captured.

29

judgement will be most beneficial to the People) as to leave you two months from this date.[1]

You will signify to your Crew that I trust it will not be necessary to continue this restrictive allowance long, and that I shall try by every means in my power to procure temporary supplys from the Enemy.[2] Meantime I am satisfied their zeal for their Country's cause will point out the absolute necessity of perservering in the Blockade of the Chesapeake to the last extremity, and that the temporary privations they are reduced to will be borne with the utmost cheerfullness.

Should the Ships' Companies and Troops express a wish to continue at full allowance of Grog while it lasts, you are at liberty to comply with their wishes in this respect, reserving a few days allowance for any extraordinary occurrances of bad weather &c.'

Add. MS. 1375.

v Cat and Mouse in the Chesapeake, November 1814.

The Chesapeake blockade involved not only harassment of American shipping attempting to leave American ports for overseas. Ships plying on internal coastal routes were also interfered with. On 10 November 1814, Captain Badcock was ordered by Captain Robert Barrie to assist in the capture of a steam vessel in regular service between Baltimore and French Town.

'The *Catch-up-a-Little* and *Little John*, Tenders to His Majesty's Ship *Dragon*, having been detached from the Squadron for the purpose of endeavouring to surprise the Steam Vessel which runs between Baltimore and French Town, and as the Enemy may send some of his Gun Vessels in pursuit of the Tenders;

It is my directions, that you proceed forthwith in the *Brune* up the Chesapeake as far as Sharps Island, for the purpose of protecting the Tenders should they be chaced, or in the event of their being successful to afford them every assistance in your power in bringing the Steam Vessel to Tangier Island off which place you will find me.

If you gain no intelligence of the Tenders within four days after your arrival off Sharps Island you will rejoin me without delay.'

Add. MS. 1375.

vi The Chesapeake blockade: American retaliation, November 1814.

American offensive tactics are revealed by the following order from Captain Robert Barrie to Captain Badcock, 23 November 1814.

'Having received Information that the Enemy has fitted out several Armed Schooners and large Row Boats for the purpose of intercepting our Tenders and transporting his Troops;

You are in Consequence to cause the most strict look out for these Vessels, and to instruct your Officers and Boats Crews to be extremely

---

[1] i.e. 'as to *last* you two months from this date'.

[2] In Badcock's published *Narrative* (*op. cit.*) he records (p. 168) treating with the Americans for food: 'We used occasionally to purchase cattle from the Americans. The plan agreed on was this: they were to drive them down to a certain point, where we were to land and take possession; for the inhabitants being all militiamen, and having too much patriotism to sell food to 'King George's men', they used to say, 'put the money under such a stone or tree . . . and then we can pick it up, and say we found it."

30

cautious how they attempt to board any of the Bay Crafts or other Vessels as the Enemy has disguised some of his Cruisers as Bay Craft.

The Row Boats are armed with heavy long Guns, and are calculated to carry about sixty Soldiers exclusive of the Crews.

An attack on Tangier Island is in contemplation, therefore the Officers on that Island are to be instructed to keep a most watchfull look out, and to be constantly prepared.'

Add. MS. 1380.

'If You Want To Live, Come Here':[1] Emigration to the United States

Crushed by poverty and the threat of destitution in Great Britain, several million emigrants crossed to America in the 19th century in search of a new land of freedom and opportunity. To the wretched and depressed, America became the symbol of hope and promise, the guarantee of cheap land and full employment, where fortunes could be made in exchange for hard work and enterprise.

Between 1835 and 1860 over two million emigrated from Great Britain to the United States, a total in excess of the number that emigrated to all the British colonies put together during the same period.[2] American statistics show that the number of people born in the United Kingdom and resident in the United States very nearly doubled in the twenty years between 1850 and 1870.[3]

What drove them to take this desperate step?

By the early 19th century vast numbers of British industrial and agricultural workers were suffering from the effects of economic forces few understood or even less could remedy. No other country in the world had experienced such a rapid and dramatic upheaval as wrought by the British Industrial and Agricultural Revolutions. Now, more than ever before, the country was at the mercy of international markets and industrial slumps and the dislocation caused by the introduction of new methods and machinery. In towns there were the Luddites, and in the country the followers of Captain Swing, both intent on the destruction of the new machinery robbing them of their jobs.[4] There was the added problem of a rising population. The combination of high prices and low wages or unemployment led to a scale of poverty and despair threatening the very fabric of society.

POVERTY IN SUSSEX

Sussex, as an agricultural county, suffered like most rural areas. In the 1830s and 40s, for example, there was massive unemployment. Those lucky enough to be in work between 1830 and 1840 could expect to earn an average weekly wage of between 10s. (50p) and 12s. (60p).[5]

i   In the early 19th century the Reverend Arthur Young published a set of statistics covering wages and the price of provisions in Sussex. In the case of Cuckfield, for example, the average wage for a six day week was 8s. (40p) or 9s. (45p) for winter and summer work respectively. Bread cost 1s. 1½d. (5½p) per peck loaf and cheese 6d. (2½p) per pound. In

<hr>

[1] From a letter by two Sussex emigrants living in New York State. This letter is quoted in this anthology, p. 41.

[2] *Thirty-third General Report of the Emigration Commissioners*, Appendix no. I (1873), quoted in Terry Coleman, *Passage to America* (1972), pp. 295–296.

[3] For 1850 and 1870 the respective numbers were 1,364,986 and 2,626,241. Quoted in E. L. Woodward, *The Age of Reform, 1815–1870* (1938), pp. 580–581.

[4] '*Machinery* is the point of contention amongst the poor, and the public should be made to know, that it is *Machinery* that is making our Ruin . . .' Henry Appleton to Charles, 5th Duke of Richmond, 2 December 1830. West Sussex Record Office, Goodwood MS. 1445 (no. 77).

[5] West Sussex Record Office, Cobden Papers 405.

other words a day's winter work (1s. 4d. per day, or 6½p) would not even buy a loaf of bread and a pound of cheese.

With these Cuckfield, and other, statistics, Young concluded:

'The high price of many of the necessaries of life is an object of great consequence: political arithmeticians and calculators have quarrelled for more than a century, whether or not the price of labour is in proportion to the price of provisions. That it should have been ever doubted is surprising.

Most clearly the wages of labouring families are inadequate to support them in that comfortable condition which they are entitled to expect: it is evident from the general increase of rates; but far more so to any man who thinks it no disgrace to visit the dwellings of the poor: their clothes, their bedding, diet, fuel, and cot; and when the interior of the cottager's house is inspected, will it be made a question whether labour and provisions are upon a par? 'Tis absurdity to question it . . .'

Rev. Arthur Young, General View of the Agriculture of the County
of Sussex (1808), pp. 406, 411, 412. (The 1813 impression,
reprinted 1970.)

THE CASH FOR EMIGRATION

Self help from private savings or the sale of personal effects took a vast number of emigrants to the United States. Others were helped by assistance either from private benefactors or from the parish rates, sometimes from a combination of both.

i   Cost of eight tickets: one house and garden.

'Memorandum: Whereas at the General Meeting of the Inhabitants of Lindfield in the County of Sussex in Vestry Assembled on the 25th Day of March 1820. It was Agreed by the Majority of the Inhabitants then Present to Assist Wm. Isted of Lindfield, Labourer, with a Sum of Money not exceeding Sixty Pounds for and towards paying his Frait Passage or Expenses of Conveying his Family consisting of Himself, Wife, and Six Children to America. And on Consideration that he the said Wm. Isted did give up all that his Messuage or Cottage Garden and Premises Situated at Scaines Hill in the said Parish of Lindfield to the Church Wardens & Overseers of the Poor of the said Parish for the time being for the use of the said Inhabitants of Lindfield for Ever. In Witness my Hand this Fourteenth day of August One Thousand Eight Hundred and Twenty. [Signed] William Isted.'

Par. 416/37/5/14/1.

ii   From Aldingbourne to New York.

The parish of Aldingbourne met the expenses of sending sixty emigrants to the United States in 1831 and 1832.[1]

The largest party—a group of thirty-eight—sailed from Portsmouth to New York in the spring of 1832 at a total cost of £400. The accounts were set out in the overseers' records:

'1832 April 27th. An Account of the expenses attending the Emigration to New York in America of Charles Southerton, his Wife and Nine Children, Namely, Thomas aged 21 years, Mary aged 19 years, Ann

---

[1] For letters from two of these Aldingbourne emigrants see below, pp. 42–43.

33

aged 16 years, Joseph aged 14 years, Harriet aged 12 years, Lydia aged 9 years, Richard aged 6 years, James aged 4 years, and Emely aged 7 months.

Also George Southerton, his Wife and Four Children, Namely, George aged 11 years, William aged 9 years, Charlotte aged 6 years, and Isaac aged 3 years.

Also John Harvey, his Wife and Six Children, Namely, William aged 12 years, Jane aged 10 years, Mary aged 7 years, John aged 5 years, James aged 3 years, and Harriet aged 1 year.

Also George White, his Wife and Five Children, Namely, Jane aged 15 years, Ann aged 13 years, George and Charles, Tweens, aged 9 years, and Edmund aged 7 years.

Also George Smart aged 20 years. Also Reuben Smart aged 18 years.

Also Joseph Peachey aged 20 years. Also James Merton aged [blank] years.

Also Thomas Bridger aged 18 years. Also Harriet Woodruff aged 19 years.

In all 38 Persons.

	£	s.	d.
1832 April 27th.			
Paid Messrs. Garratt and Gibbon for the Passage of the above 38 Emigrants to New York.	165	0	0
Paid William Bayley a Bill for Grocery for ye above.	21	2	10
Paid G. Gray a Bill for Biscuit, Flour &c.	11	0	0
Paid Wm. Owen a Bill for 7 Beds and Blankets.	4	4	0
Paid R. Atlee a Bill for Potatoes.	1	11	9
Paid E. Cole a Bill for Board and lodging for the above 38 Persons.	8	6	8
Paid the above 38 Emigrants £3. pr. Head bounty.	114	0	0
Paid Charles Southerton in lieu for his own meat.	4	7	0
Paid George Southerton in lieu for Do. Do.	2	5	6
Paid George White in lieu for Do. Do.	2	14	6
Paid James Arthur and Charles Millyard for the Conveyance of the above 38 Emigrants to Portsmouth.	4	0	0
Paid the above 38 Emigrants expenses on the road to Portsmouth.	2	0	0
John Burnand and Edmund Boniface's expenses to and from Portsmouth, absent three days.[1]	4	10	0
Sept. 27th.			
Paid Messrs. Sowton and Fuller a Bill for Preparing Bond from Richd. Hasler Esqr. and others, for the Securement of Four Hundred Pounds and Interest, to Mr. George Prior, Borrowed for the Purpose of sending the above Emigrants to New York in America. Procuration Fee, Stamp £4, and attendance &c.	6	0	0
Octr. 3rd.			
Paid the Residue of the above Four Hundred Pounds Borrowed of Mr. George Prior into the Bank of Messrs. Ridge &c. at Chichester.	48	17	9
	400	0	0'

Par. 1/30/1.

[1] Burnand and Boniface were the Overseers of the Poor for Aldingbourne.

iii   From Ireland to New York.

The failure of the Irish potato crop in 1845 and 1846 brought famine to Ireland on a scale unparalleled in the country's history. Between 1847 and 1855 the total number of Irish entering New York was 892,000 compared with 299,000 from England, Scotland and Wales.[1]

One of the more responsible absentee landlords at the time of the famine was George James, 6th Earl of Egmont of Cowdray in Sussex who owned the Lohort Castle estate in County Cork. He gave relief, provided work and assisted emigration. In 1847 he met the following expenses in sending Michael Denalry and his family to New York on the *Liberty* from Liverpool.

	£	s.	d.
'To Cash paid expense of the family to Cork per Car.	0	17	6
To Cash for Clothes (they being really in rags).	4	0	0
To Cash for Passage of 8 persons to New York by Liverpool.	35	10	0
To Cash to provide sea store.	5	10	0
To Cash to support them in Liverpool from their arrival there till sailing of the vessel. 5 days at 1s. each	2	0	0
To Cash for use in America while looking for employment	2	2	6
Total	50	0	0'

Cowdray MS. 1914 (no. 24).

iv   '. . . wants to go to America': applications to West Grinstead Vestry.

There was considerable poverty and distress in the parish of West Grinstead in the 1830s. The parish officers received a number of applications for financial assistance to emigrate to the United States. Some of the entries recorded in the Vestry Minute Book are as follows:

	'Applications, Orders, &c. as Follows	Order'd
1834 9 Dec.	James Parsons & Mathew Caffin wants to go to America if the Parish will Pay their Expenses and gave [*recte* give] a few Shillings to have after they gets there.	Left till another Vestry.
23 Dec.	James Parsons & Mathew Caffin wants to go to America if the Parish will pay their Expenses, and £5 each after they gets there.	Apply to Mr. Woodward & Sir C. M. Burrell.[2]
1835 6 Jan.	James Parsons has spoken to Mr. Woodward respecting going to America, and Mr. Woodward will Speak to Sir C. M. Burrell, & Mrs. Gorin,[2] and he sais no doubt but they will Subscribe sumething, and he will do the best he can, and he hopes the Parish will do the same. Mathew Caffin has given up going.	—

---

[1] *Annual Reports of the Commissioners of Emigration of the State of New York, 1847–60*, Table A, quoted in Terry Coleman, *op. cit.*, pp. 297–298.
[2] The Rev. W. P. Woodward, Rector of West Grinstead. Sir Charles Merrick Burrell of Knepp Castle, Shipley, and Mrs. Mary Goring of Wiston Park, were the principal landowners in West Grinstead.

3 March	James Parsons wants £28 for him & his Wife and two Children to go to America. Mr. Woodward wishes to know how much the Parish will Allow him, then Mr. Woodward will see Sir C. Burrell & Mrs. Goring to know if they will join with him to make up the remainder.	£21.
17 March	John Bristow, Wife & 4 Children, wants the Parish to pay their Expenses to America.	£35.
14 April	Henry Short [of] Storrington, wants the Parish Officers to pay his Expenses to America, and give him Two or three Pounds to put in his Pocket when he gets to America.	—
	James Parsons wants the Parish to give him 5 or 6 pounds for Pocket Money when he gets to America.	—
28 April	Henry Short [of] Storrington wants the Parish officers to pay his Expenses to America, & 2 or 3 Pounds for Pocket Money.'	—

Par. 95/12/1.

v   From Ditchling to America: a cry for help.

'To the Gentry and Inhabitants of Ditchling, its Vicinity and the Benevolent Public.

George and Harriet Verrall, the master & mistress of the Ditchling National Schools most earnestly implore the means of enabling them to Emigrate to America with eight Children (being those out of 13), now entirely dependent on the reduced master & mistress's Salary of fifteen Shillings a week for their maintenance.

Your Petitioners apply First Because they have received Notice that the limited Fund at the disposal of the Committee will not enable them to keep on the Schools as at present and that the master and mistress must leave at Michaelmas next.

Secondly, Because G. & H. Verrall would then have no other means of support or prospect of any in England with their large Infant Family, that being encouraged by their Son Walter, who Emigrated to America in August last (through the benevolence of the Charitable), to come if possible to him with all his unprovided for Brothers and Sisters, as each would there be able to earn a something towards the support of the Family. They are most anxious to emigrate with all their Children and ready cheerfully to undergo all hardships and privations and to embark on the shortest notice when their passage money amounting to the sum of Sixty Pounds shall be secured.

Thirdly, That the Inhabitants of Ditchling and its Vicinity having contributed towards the Passage of their Son Walter and afforded much kindness to them, G. Verrall & his Wife, they are most anxious to emigrate forthwith that they may not be compelled to apply to the Parish for Parochial Relief. Therefore they entreat the Gentry & Inhabitants of Ditchling and the benevolent Public to subscribe at the foot of this Petition their Names and the sums they will kindly promise

to pay to Jno. Attree Esqre. of Ditchling, on his being satisfied that with
the Assistance which your Petitioner & his Wife hope to get, through
a petition placed in the hands of Mr. Wm. Homewood at Lindfield,
the amount of Passage money will be forth coming when required to
be paid, before which time no money will be asked for.'

There then follows a list of promised subscriptions and the following
memorandum:

'Novr. 1853. As the promised Subscriptions did not amount even to
half the requisite sum, the Emigration of the Family in 1853 was
unavoidably given up. This was so far fortunate, as the Father received
another letter from his son in America earnestly beseeching him not to
think of Coming out in the Winter but to come whenever it could be
managed in the Spring of the year. The Schools have since been kept
open by the Subscribers and G.V. & his family continue in the house
with an understanding that all the Family are to go to America according to their wishes in April next (1854). Under these circumstances it
has been arranged by G.V.'s friends that to insure the family going at
that time (or as many of them as the funds will then admit of) the
Ladies and Gentlemen who have kindly agreed by this paper to
contribute should be requested forthwith to pay their Subscriptions to
Mr. J. Attree who will acknowledge the receipt and that G. Verrall
should solicit fresh Subscriptions to be also placed in the hands of Mr.
Jno. Attree who will see that the Money shall be carefully applied to
secure their Passage of as many of the Family as the Funds will admit of.
For their sake and to save them from destitution it is to be hoped it will
amount to the £60. G. Verrall is to solicit the Humane and Benevolent
to subscribe their names and residences at the foot of this Additional
Subscription paper and to call on Mr. J. Attree from time to time that
he may know the state of the Fund, G.V. paying to him each time of
calling such money as Subscribers may find it more convenient to pay
through him and obtaining Mr. Jno. Attree's receipt hereon for the
satisfaction of all Subscribers. In the Spring those Ladies & Gentlemen
who have aided this distressed family to accomplish by Emigration the
object of their Ambition, that of earning their own living & avoiding
the disgrace of applying for Parochial relief, will be made acquainted
with the appropriation and result of their Subscriptions.'

There then follows a further list of promised subscriptions.

Par. 416/37/5/14/2.

ACROSS THE ATLANTIC: THE VOYAGE

Most emigrants bound for the United States sailed from either Liverpool
or London, although many smaller ports such as Portsmouth and Rye
were used.[1]

The average run of emigrant ships was appalling, and steerage passengers, paying the minimum rates for their tickets, could suffer terrible
ordeals.

'Before the emigrant has been a week at sea he is an altered man. How
can it be otherwise? Hundreds of poor people, men, women, and children,

---

[1] For example, the Aldingbourne families who emigrated to New York (see above, pp.
33–34) sailed from Portsmouth. Official British government figures show that 1,416
emigrants sailed from Rye to the United States between 1828 and 1830. West Sussex
Record Office, Goodwood MS. 641.

of all ages, from the drivelling idiot of ninety to the babe just born, huddled together without light, without air, wallowing in filth and breathing a fetid atmosphere, sick in body, dispirited in heart, the fevered patients lying between the sound, in sleeping places so narrow as almost to deny them the power of indulging, by a change of position, the natural restlessness of the disease; by their agonised ravings disturbing those around, and predisposing them, through the effects of the imagination, to imbibe the contagion; living without food or medicine, except as administered by the hand of casual charity, dying without the voice of spiritual consolation, and buried in the deep without the rites of the church.'[1]

Although food was provided for steerage passengers it was generally uncooked. The emigrants could use the ships' stoves as best they could. They were recommended to take additional rations and basic equipment such as bedding and cooking utensils which could often be bought at the last moment at the quayside.

LAST MINUTE SHOPPING

i   When William Tourle and his family emigrated from West Grinstead to New York in 1849 they did their last minute shopping for the voyage at J. B. Whyte's *General Provision Warehouse* by St. Katherine's Docks, London. The surviving bill—paid for by the parish—shows the range of goods sold to emigrants. The items shown with an asterisk* were those bought by the Tourles.

Tea	Soda	Coverlids
Coffee	Candles*	Provision Chests*
Cocoa	Vinegar*	Bottled Ale
Sugar	Pickles	Bottled Porter
Loaf Sugar	Oranges	Saucepans*
Tobacco*	Lemons	Fryingpans
Hams*	Oatmeal	Plates
Bacon*	Packets of Groats	Mugs
Corned Beef	Barley	Dishes
Pickled Pork	Peas	Wash Bowls
Pickled Tongues	Fine Biscuit	Chambers*
Suet	Second Biscuit	Slop Pails
Butter*	Loaves of Bread	Water Bottles*
Lard*	Rusked Bread	Hook Pots*
Eggs	Flour	Lanterns*
Cheese*	Herrings	Tea Pots
Raisins*	Potatoes*	Port
Currants	Onions	Sherry
Rice	German Sausages	Brandy*
Spices	Knives and Forks	Rum[2]
Mustard*	Spoons	Geneva
Pepper*	Nets*	Pipes
Salt*	Sea Beds*	
Soap*	Blankets	

Par. 95/38/7.

---

[1] Letter from Stephen de Vere in *First Report from the Select Committee of the House of Lords on Colonisation from Ireland*, H.C., 1847–8, vol. 17.

[2] For the Tourles' bill the item for rum has been deleted and another item, which is illegible, written in its place.

EMIGRATION POSTERS

Posters distributed by the emigration commissioners and the emigration and shipping agents were posted up throughout the length and breadth of the British Isles. 'The posters were stuck up in Irish villages too, though many of the Irish could not speak English, let alone read it. One reporter, who was a Scot and therefore could read, said it was sadly clear that the inmates of the cottages on which the posters appeared knew little more of their meaning than if they had been Chinese notices on a tea-chest.'[1]

i   A printed 19th century poster advertising emigration to Western Virginia is reproduced in this anthology. The original was sent to the parish authorities of West Grinstead. See plate no. III.

Par. 95/38/7.

'EVERY THING IS PLENTY, AND VERY CHEAP . . .':[2]
THE NEW LIFE

Life in the new country was harsh but abundantly rewarding to all those who persevered. On British standards the opportunities were unlimited to those prepared to take up the challenge. There was plenty of employment and higher wages, land at ridiculously cheap prices, and food was both cheap and plentiful. Apart from the gossip, this was the message of so many letters sent home to family and friends by emigrants, and was the message exploited by many who wished to encourage further emigration. Collections of these letters were made and published as a form of emigration propaganda. Other propaganda extolling the prosperity awaiting the emigrant was published in the form of printed leaflets. Some examples of this type of propaganda are reproduced below.[3]

i   Letter from George Grevatt, formerly of Sullington, now in Detroit, 30 March 1828.

'Dear Brother,
 . . . After a voyage of 7 weeks we arrived at New York, at getting on board of another boat, we travelled 800 miles and arrived at Detroit, we are much pleased with this country, and are very happily situated in the family of Mr. Jones with whom we have lived ever since we have been in this country: we live in the house and sleep here too: I get 22s. a week[4] and my wife 10s. land is very cheap, we have got 60 acres of land and have got 5 acres cleared, and we expect to build us a house next fall: you thought that the land in this country was very poor, but it is rich and heavy timbered. I think that you could do well in this country if you felt disposed to come. Flour is only 5s. a bushel, and tea that you pay 12s. for we get here for five, soap and candles you can have for the making, and wood to draw it away, and those who are too lazy to draw it can get it for 7 shillings a load, beef and pork is about 3 pence a pound, brandy is about 14 pence a quart, and whiskey about 6 pence, and a man's wages by the day 4 shillings and a sixpence: and found this country is somewhat colder than England, but wood is so plenty that

---

[1] Terry Coleman, *op. cit.*, p. 56.
[2] From the letter by George Grevatt transcribed below.
[3] The printed letters that follow (nos. i–iv) are taken from photostat copies held by the West Sussex Record Office.
[4] In the same year, 1828, the average weekly wage for a male farm worker in Sussex was 12s. (60p). West Sussex Record Office, Cobden Papers 405.

we do not feel it. I do not wish to urge you too much to come, yet, I feel that it would be for your advantage, and if any young girls or men want good places that they had better come here, and if John Barnard or Richard Butcher wants to come, it would be a good thing for them, and let them bring two or three good boys or girls and I could get them good places where they can get 5s. and 6d. a week: there is a lady here spoke to me to send for a good girl for her, and I shall take care that she is well provided for, and when I have a house of my own, she shall call it her home when she has no place. The girls in this country are not called servants but hired help, & have a great many privileges; & if John Barnard comes, I wish that he would bring Eleanor Murfee: it will cost about 12 pounds and a half to come as far as we have: some people think it a pleasure to come over the sea, and others are very sick; if you come you had better bring plenty of rice and groats, in case you are sick: we had to wait a week in London before the vessel was ready to sail, and we were quite sea sick, and was glad that I had a little wine and something to make gruel. We intended to write sooner, but have neglected it, and we feel so well pleased, we thought best to write, and you may depend that we have told you the truth, and nothing but the truth, as we promised: We never have heard from you since we have been here; you must write to us as soon as possible, and write all the news. We wish to hear from you very much: the most of my wife's relations have come here; my father and six brothers; my father and my brother came out last spring. Allen and his wife and four children came when we did. Allen has bought land, and built him a house of his own. Sarah and myself expect to go to see them soon. I am sure if you would come, that you would be very much pleased with this country: it is very pleasant, and every thing is plenty, and very cheap; and we have a great many vegetables and things that you never saw or heard tell of, and it is healthy. I have been very well since I have been here, but Sarah has not been for some time. There is a great deal of difference in the money, the money here is less: one shilling of English money is eleven pence more than our shillings, & 8 shillings make a dollar. Give our best respects to Mrs. Butcher, Mrs. Woods, Mrs. Fain, and tell them they must write to us, and write all the news. Give our love to Dame Murser . . . You must copy this letter, and send it to William King, Javington.[1] Give our love to your wife, and all our enquiring friends, and accept the same from me your brother.

GEORGE GREVATT.

Sarah has learnt to make bread without yeast, and without an oven: we are above 4000 miles from home.'

The publisher has added 'This person sold his furniture and went from Sullington at his own expence'.

M.P. 1070.

ii   Letter from George and Jane Kimber, formerly of Horsted Keynes, now in Pittsford, New York State, 6 December 1829.

This letter was published in the same booklet as the letter from George Grevatt, printed above.

---

[1] Jevington in Sussex.

'Dear father and mother.

. . . If you want to live, come here; for I can have meat three times a day now, where I could not get a little piece for a sunday's dinner: now I will tell you the price of the things of this country; you can have wheat at 6s. to 6s. and 6d. a bushel, of this money, that is, 3s. to 3s. and 3d. your money; oats at 1s. per bushel, corn 2s. per bushel, beef at 2d. per pound, mutton 1½d. per pound. Prints be rather dearer here than there, and so is grocery, geese at 6d, turkeys at 2s. of your money, each. I am now living in my friend Thomas Ockenden's house, and he is my friend, for he gives me a good many privileges, and he is a good friend to me. We had a very pleasant voyage over the water, and up to Albany, but you may tell Thomas Homan, that I had only 1s. 3d. of your money when I had paid my affairs. I had only one friend with me, and that was Mr. ——; but never mind now, for I shall do. I had 12 dollars a month, and all my board and firing found me, and now I work any where, and I make more of my time now, for here is two three and four comes for me a day, and I get all round as fast as I can. I should like to see some or all of you next spring. I do not want to persuade you to come, but come if you like, and stop if you like: I know who has got the best home, and if you think of coming, you let me know soon enough, that I may write to you, to let you know what I want you to bring, and what is best for you to bring: do not you mind what people say to you, but let me know if any of you mean to come: you must not mind what people say, about letters being forged,[1] for it is no such thing, I can assure you; but it is no use of your thinking to come here to live without work; but if you mind your own business, and keep yourself from drinking, you may do well, and all the people will respect you, and help you; but an idle or drunken person is looked upon about as well as a mad dog, and no one will help them. A man may have as much drink as will do him good, but let him mind his business, and then he will do well. Give our kind love to all our friends, and tell them that we like the place very well, too well to come back again. Do not be mad because I have not mentioned all your names, but this letter is to all, and when you write to me, direct Mr. George Kimber, at Mr. Thomas Ockenden's, Pittsford, Monrow County, State of New York, North America. So no more at present, we remain your affectionate son and daughter, brother and sister, GEORGE and JANE KIMBER.'

The publisher has added 'George Kimber went from Horsted Keynes: his wife's maiden name was Botting, and her mother resides at Washington, Sussex'.

M.P. 1070.

---

[1] There were accusations that many of the letters from emigrants were forgeries designed to misrepresent the conditions. Writing of letters received from Canadian emigrants, the Rev. T. Sockett of Petworth referred to 'many curious devices' used to guard against such fraud. 'The paper on which letters from Canada were to be written, was prepared in England, either by a heading in the hand of a friend, a name written across, certain mystical holes pricked with a pin, or, what was more general, a sort of tally, formed by a corner of the paper being scrawled upon, and then torn off, the piece torn away being carefully preserved at home. In one instance, a very small, and peculiarly shaped, crooked pin, placed under the seal, came back from the *'far west'*; with especial directions, that this infallible proof should be again returned thither. These directions have been complied with, and the crooked pin, is now once more on its voyage.' Quoted from *Emigration: Letters from Sussex Emigrants, who sailed from Portsmouth, in April 1832, on board the ships, Lord Melville and Evaline, for Upper Canada . . .* (1833), p. viii.

The following two letters were published by the Poor Law Commissioners in 1834. Both writers emigrated with their families from Aldingbourne in 1832. The expenses for their emigration are referred to in the Aldingbourne parish accounts. See above, pp. 33–34.

iii   Letter from Charles Southerton, formerly of Aldingbourne, now in Cross Roads, near New Brunswick, New Jersey, 19 September 1832.

'Dear Father and Mother,

. . . I am very happy and I think Providence smiles upon me. I am at work at ditching at present and get a dollar a day . . . and when we have done ditching there is plenty of woodcutting. a steady man might hearn 6s. a day[1] which I have ever since I have been here and sometimes more . . . If any of you should come (I never will persuade no one) when they do come, bring spades and shovels and handbills, for there is none in this country, and large wooden bottles. Ripe Hooks is but little service for they cradle all their corn hear . . . If people knowed what America was, they never (would) stay in old England. We was 7 weeks and 1 day upon our voyage . . . we past 5 ice burgs in 1 day, they are as large as any barn . . . There is plenty of Peach orchards, they 1 dollar a bushel; and plenty of apples, they are 10 cents a bushel . . .

Mr Southerton	Your dutifull and affecte. son
Alingbourn	Chas. Southerton.'
Sussex	

iv   Letter from John Harvey, formerly of Aldingbourne, now in Lysander, New York State, 10 February 1833.

'Dear friends,

. . . We were very happy and comfortable, and I have plenty of employment for this winter season. I am chiefly threshing for which I get the 10th bushel of all kind of grain and our board; it is the custom of the country to be boarded and lodged, let you work at what you will; and tradesmen the same; and Master and Mistress and all the family sit all at 1 table, and if there is not room at the table for the whole family to sit down, their children sit by till workmen were served; there is no distinction between the workman and his master, they would as soon shake hands with a workman as they would with a gentleman. My boy and I can thresh from 10 to 12 bushels pr day of wheat, and as for the summer season we find plenty of cuting new ditches through the swamps, at which I can arn from a dollar to 10s. per day. This country requires a man as can make himself handy at jobing; a man that can do nothing but go with horses will not stand so good a chance, as the farmer generally go with his horses or oxen himself, except now and then one will hire a single man by the month for which he will get from 10 to 12 dollars per month, washing and mending; there is no difficulty of a man's getting along in this country if he is industress, but it is not of any service to a man to come here to think of living independent without work, for the farmer has to work and till the land himself. So now I will give you an account of the different prices of provishons and land—

---

[1] This pay of 6s. (30p) per day should be compared to the average weekly wage for a farm labourer in Sussex in the same year, 1832. This was 12s. (60p). See Cobden Papers 405. The following letter quoted here indicates that it was possible to earn as much as 10s. (50p) per day in New York State in the summer months.

wheat is 1 dollar pr bushel, India corn from 4s. to 4s. 6d. oates from
2s. 6d. to 3s. barley is from 4s. to 6s. per bushel and pork by the hog
from 3½d. to 4d. per lb. mutton 3d. beef from 3d. to 4d. butter 1s.
cheese 6d. sugar 1od; and as for live stock, a good cow for 20 dollars, a
fat sheep about 2 dollars, lean hogs from 2½d. to 3d. per lb., a yoke of
cattle from 45 to 65 dollars; and as for land you may buy at 20 dollars
per acre improved, timber land from 3 dollars to 7; it depends upon
where it is situated; there is no difficulty of a man's geting of land here
if he is industrious and temperate in drink, and have a good character;
many will let a man have land with a few acres improvement and a
house on it without any deposit, by paying interest for the time he
contract for it, and will give you 5 or 6 years to pay the principle in by
installments. Clothing is somewhat higher than in England. I wish
shoes were cheaper, I wish some good shoemaker would come out, as
the shoemakers were very indifferent hands here, and there is a man
a collar maker has made application to me to write for a man of that
branch, he will give him after the rate of a guinea pr week and his
board and washing and mending, and if he is a good workman after a
time he will give him more. When I was in England I thought it a very
fine thing if I could get on Cr.mas day 3 or 4lb. of beef, but this year I
killed a steer supposed to way 88 stun, and I had tallow enough to
make candels to last all the year, and I sold the skin 3½ dollars, and I
gave 20 dollars for it . . . I think God my wife and I never found ourselves so comfortable in England as we do here, we have a good
comfortable house to live in, and a good cow for our use, and a plenty
of firing without buying fuel, we don't go to bed with a hungery belly
nor sit a cold . . .

To Mrs. James Modey   Your well wisher
Aldinbourn   John Harvey.'
nr Chichester.

*The First Report from the Commissioners on the Poor Laws, Appendix
C, Parliamentary Papers, 1834, vol. 37, pp. 157–158.*[1]

v   Illinois: 'a bilious Aguish and religious Country'.

Letter from William Atkinson, formerly of London, now in Peoria,
Illinois, 8 March 1850.

'Dear Friend,

I take this opportunity in answer to yours of Novr. 1848, though many
months has elapsed since I received your letter. I hope you did not give
up all idea of hearing from me again had an early answer been required.
I should have been more prompt. I shall ever as the duty of a Friend
write you occasionally to keep up and renew old acquaintanship, and I
hope not at such long intervals. You desire to know what kind of
country we are associated in. It is a bilious Aguish and religious Country.
I guess it is the same althrough America except in large Towns. This
Country is in the Far West and like [in] all new settled Countries
dwells [sicknesses] such as Bilious Fevers, Agues. We have nothing to
complain of with regard to health with the exception of Father. He
had the Ague all one Winter. The rest of us has had first rate Health.

---

[1] There is a further series of letters from a Sussex emigrant covering the period 1794–
1819 in two articles by David Mclean: 'John Burgess of Ditchling and America' in
Sussex County Magazine, vol. 11 (1937), pp. 657–662, 694–699.

As the Country gets more settled these diseases will be rare. Let me try to tell you what the Ague is. When you are attacked you will shake and tremble with cold from 45 to 30 minutes. Then [it] turns to a fever . . . It generally attacks one every other Day . . . Society here is not so agreeable as in London. We have no parks, Gardens, Theatres or public Lectures such as we use[d to] frequently attend. We are somewhat accustomed to the manners and Customs of this country and think little about such recreation . . .

Thomas, If you and Anne have any idea of coming to America you had better go to some large Town such as New York, Baltimore or Philadelphia . . .

If you are desirous of going on land I should suggest to you the Potters Emigration Society. I believe it is the best that a poor man can belong to. If I recollect right each member has 10 acres of land (at government price 4 shillings and 2 pence per acre, with 2 acres improved, a log House & 18 months provisions) by the payment of 6d. per week[1]. . . You have 10 years to pay to the Society the expense they have incurred in improving your land. Thomas, I want you to inquire about this Society, how it is progressing and whether a man or party in America can join, and where they are located.

Thomas, my history will be brief. Since I have been in America I have been Jack of all Trades. I am now Waiter in a Hotel.

Jane is a housemaid, Mary the same and they are doing first rate.

If you call on Mr. Lawley, 18 Red Lion Court, Spital Field [London] he may give you some information about the Potters Emigration Society, as I have some notion of buying a piece of land . . .

There is plenty of Government Land here suitable to co-operators without going so far north as Wisconsin, within 200 miles of St. Louis on or near the Mississippi River. You can farm here with less expense than so far north for their long Winters takes heap of labour to grow feed for stock.

The Cattle taken to the prairies picks up their own food as long as their [is] any grass.

Quincy, a town on the upper Mississippi, is the land office for this State (Illinois) where parties can learn where there is Government Land.

The French Communists or Icarians are at Navoo, Illinois.[2] They seem to go along pretty well together. I read an account of some Irish Catholics coming to this Country buying 2,000 acres of Government land about 300 miles below St. Louis on the Mississippi. I hear the Chartists Land has failed.[3] Is it so?

<table>
<tr><td>Our address Peoria</td><td>Your Respected Friend,</td></tr>
<tr><td>Illinois,</td><td>Wm. Atkinson.</td></tr>
<tr><td>United States of America.</td><td></td></tr>
</table>

---

[1] Or, at 21p per acre, paying back 2½p per week.

[2] The French Communists, or Icarians, of Nauvoo were the followers of the French Communist Etienne Cabet (1788–1856). Their first settlement—an attempt to set up the perfect commonwealth in Texas—had failed. Their second attempt at Nauvoo, Illinois, although apparently successful to the writer of this letter in 1850, also failed soon after.

[3] The English Chartists who were agitating for political reform in the 1830s and 40s established the National Land Company in 1847 to make land available to the working man. Although estates were purchased and several thousands of pounds collected from weekly subscriptions, the scheme failed and the company was finally dissolved in 1851.

P.S. Write Soon. Give us all the news you can & remember me to all inquiring Friends. W.A.'

The letter bears the name and address of Mr. Thomas Bloomfield, in the care of Mrs. Moss, 5 Fountain Court, Strand, London, England. A short note to Bloomfield by Jane Atkinson has been added to the letter.

Add. MS. 10,910.

vi   'Kansas . . . Valuable Information for British Farmers'.

Printed leaflet, published *c.* 1880, advertising land for sale and the advantages of emigration to Kansas. For the illustrated cover page showing 'before' and 'after' cultivation scenes see plate no. IV.

Sections include details relating to soils, climate, crops, cattle and sheep raising, herd law, markets, the cost of building a house, the credit terms for the purchase of land, fuel, prices for basic farm equipment, schools, churches and emigration. There is a map, and engravings of a Kansas home, a rolling prairie scene, and a 'Mennonite settlement in Harvey County, Kansas, one year from the raw prairie' and another giving 'the same, after four years' work and improvements'. There are also advertisements for Santa Fe, 'The Jerusalem of America', for 'The Celebrated Hot Springs of Las Vegas' and 'The Richest Gold Fields and Silver Mines of Colorado, New Mexico and Arizona' which could all be reached by the Atchison, Topeka & Santa Fe Rail Road Company.

Some selected extracts from this leaflet are as follows:

'Cattle Raising in Chase and Marion Counties. What £1,000 Will Do.

It will purchase a farm of 320 acres, one-third rich bottom land in the valley, balance high rolling pasture land, for £250. It will pay for a small house costing £150, a team costing £40, harness £10, wagon £15, for fences about the house and yards, corrals and sheds, costing £40; for 50 head of native two-year-old heifers, costing £3.12s. each, or £180; two Durham bulls, costing £60, for incidental expenses in support of family until crop is raised, £100—leaving a balance of £150 for emergencies.

All the necessaries for home consumption can be raised on the farm, and enough sold to provide groceries, clothing, etc. The farm should be devoted principally to raising winter feed for stock. In addition to tame grasses, nutritious prairie hay can be contracted put up for 10s. per ton, and costing much less if done by the stock raiser himself. Properly handled, the breeding herd should give 80 per cent. increase each year . . . By judicious and careful breeding a well-bred herd can soon be secured; and while the improvement in the herd is going on an equal improvement should be made on the farm and home. At the end of six years fruit trees should be in bearing and fruit plentiful. Shade trees should make the home cozy and cheerful-looking; the farm should be well improved and fenced, and some of the prairie sod should by this time be converted into blue-grass and timothy pasture for early and late grazing . . .

With ordinary care and business management, stock raising in the Cottonwood Valley counties will pay $33\frac{1}{3}$ per cent. on the investment. With extra care and good management, 50 per cent. can be realized, besides the enhancement on the value of the land.

General Information

Taxes in Kansas are assessed for State, county, township, city and school purposes. All are collected by the county treasurers. Taxes for the current year are payable, one-half in December and one-half in June following. If all paid in December, a discount of two and one-half per cent. is allowed. Taxes average from one to two per cent. of actual valuation. The school tax is usually the heaviest; county taxes are usually for public improvements, and township taxes for roads, bridges, etc.

A section of land is one square mile, and contains 640 acres. This is again divided into four quarters . . . Each quarter-section, or 160 acres, can be again divided into 40-acre tracts. A township is six miles square, and contains 36 sections.

Each section line in Kansas is by law a highway . . .

No part of the United States so much resembles England as Southern Central Kansas, because of the fine hedge fences so common there, giving the fields very much the appearance of those in rural England . . .

Nearly every farmer owns the farm he works, in Kansas. One year's rent of a farm in England will buy a good farm in Kansas, and it will give a larger percentage of profit for the amount of labor put into it than will the English farm . . .

Making butter for the western market is perhaps the most profitable business in Kansas today, giving even better returns than sheep, but requiring more hard work.

Lazy men don't succeed well in Kansas. It takes hard work, push and intelligence to farm successfully here as elsewhere.

There are no Indians in Kansas. All the tribes were removed from the State to the Territories ten years ago, and there is no more danger from this source now than in New York or London.

The people of Kansas are intelligent, industrious, law-abiding and moral. They believe in schools, and support them liberally. Most of them are fairly educated and many of them well. A piano is often met with in farm houses in Kansas, and good libraries are frequent.

English farmers coming here, will find perhaps a larger percentage of intelligent farmers in a community than they will leave behind them in England.

Emigration

Every succeeding year demonstrates more clearly the fact that the American west must eventually become the chief supply source of the material necessities of life for densely populated Europe. The facilities for producing cheaply: meat, breadstuffs, fruit, dairy products, &c., are so vast and rapidly increasing with extending means of communication, and the means of cheap transportation to the seaport and thence to England and the Continent of Europe are so plentiful and perfect, ever increasing as the necessities require, that the chances for successful competition on the part of the old countries, especially of England, become more and more problematic. It is well for the British farmer to look the matter straight in the face, to study the facts and draw his own conclusions. All the patriotic suggestions for the would-be national economist, so freely offered through the press and at meetings of agricultural societies—all the remedies proposed in the interest of the farming communities at home will avail nothing as against the natural course of development in that world beyond the sea, which seems to have been 'laid by' as it were, by Providence for the present emergency of too crowded a population in too small a world. During the next centuries the vast and rich country between the Mississippi and the Rocky Mountains will be the granary of the world, whatever changes later ages may bring about. Yet the development of that region is in its first stage. Take the State of Kansas alone—a small fraction of that immense area . . . hardly one-seventh of the 52 million acres of this State is under cultivation . . . Six-sevenths of this State is yet awaiting the plough to swell the annual yield gradually to seven times that quantity! . . . England is essentially a commercial and manufacturing nation. To maintain her supremacy as such she must have cheap food. The settlement of the cheap lands of the great West and devoting them to agriculture by English people will cheapen food for England and at the same time will furnish a healthful outlet for a portion of her surplus population. Many far sighted business men and capitalists have already acted upon that conviction and have transferred capital to the West and employed it in the development of the country and in trade. Prudent English landlords have purchased large tracts of land there, anticipating a great rise in its value for the near future. Yet the individual tenant farmer has been slow to realise his interest. He plots along from year to year, making a bare living and in many instances losing of his substance; paying annually as much money in *rent* and for *fertilizers* as would purchase in Kansas a freehold farm, one that needs no manure for half a century to come . . .'

M.P. 135.

EMIGRANTS IN DISTRESS

New York was the principal port of entry for emigrants to the United States. Whilst many merely passed through the city on their way to destinations inland, many others, without money or direction, were gradually sucked under, swelling a city population which more than doubled—from 313,000 to 630,000—in the fifteen years between 1840 and 1855. 'And here is exhibited so sickening a picture of human destitution and suffering as no pen, however eloquent in the sad gloom of misfortune's description, could well paint in illustration of the dark and solemn truth. The deplorable infirmity of their desolate unhappiness must be *seen and felt* to be appreciated; and then, to often find amid the motley groups some with the last gasp of expiration issuing from their cold and blanched lips, forms a scene of dismay and distress too agonising to look upon with any other than feelings of horror and overwhelming sympathy.'[1] All too easy they became the prey of pickpockets, racketeers and crooks. Various charitable societies offered at least some relief, such as the New York Magdalen Female Benevolent Society, the New York Association for the Improvement of the Condition of the Poor, and the British Protective Emigrant Society.

i   One such organisation, the St. George's Society of New York, published an appeal leaflet to further its work in 1835.

---

[1] Letter from New York City Almshouse Commissioners, 20 July 1847, quoted in Terry Coleman, *op. cit.*, p. 160.

'The great claim on the members, and on those who may, by becoming members or in any other way, enjoy the privilege of doing good, is—*their countryman in distress—a stranger in a strange land*, and although few have it in their power to relieve every case, to the credit of humanity be it said, fewer still is the number of those who can look on such a scene with cold indifference. It need hardly here be stated, that the cases which call for charitable aid are numerous and various. Those who, urged by philanthropy, or in their course of their duty as officers of some charitable association, have made a winter's walk through the narrow streets and by-lanes of this large city, those and those only can duly appreciate the value of a few dollars, or what good even a single dollar may sometimes effect in the garret, the cellar, and the hovel, when properly distributed and seasonably applied. It is not so much the common beggar, whose home is in every street and at every body's door, who claims the attention of the charitable committee; it is more frequently the silent sufferer, who has seen better days; assistance to whom, when administered with delicacy, comes nearer the heart of both him who gives and him who receives . . .

When it is known that the whole amount of the available funds proceeds from the interest of eleven shares of United States bank stock, and the annual payments of five dollars each, from about one hundred and thirty subscribers, it will be seen that the sum distributed is but small. And when it is recollected that immigration has greatly increased, it will be evident to a common observer, that the calls on the Society have increased in a far greater ratio than the means for relief. To Englishmen visiting the United States for either profit or pleasure, an appeal on behalf of their countrymen in distress is respectfully made. To Englishmen at home, who may have commercial or other interests in common with this country, an opportunity is afforded of enjoying a consciousness that they have administered to the sick, fed the hungry, clothed the naked—their own countrymen, who have left their native land to seek a living on a distant shore . . .'

Cobden Papers 394.

Slavery

Negro slavery in America can be traced back to the early 17th century when Africans were first imported for forced labour in the new colonial settlements. As these settlements developed—particularly in the Southern colonies with the growth of the large cotton plantations—the need for slavery expanded. By the 18th century the whole fabric of Southern society had become totally dependent on a slave economy for its prosperity.

In the early 19th century the number of slaves in the Southern states of the new republic was growing. Britain's Industrial Revolution and its insatiable demand for raw cotton, coupled with the invention of Whitney's cotton gin which made further expansion of the cotton estates possible, intensified the need for more labour still further. To keep pace with the new demands, the South's 'peculiar institution' was seen as 'so necessary that it ceased to appear evil'.[1] As production and exports leapt forward to satisfy the new markets, the number of slaves increased between 1820 and 1860 from $1\frac{1}{4}$ to 4 millions. In 1859 the British Consul in New York reported that he found 'the African Slave Trade is being prosecuted with more vigor than for years past . . . the flag of the U.S. [is] the great promoter & protector of the traffic'.[2]

NEWSPAPER ADVERTISEMENTS

Newspapers published in the South clearly reveal the existence of slavery as quite a normal part of everyday life. The advertisements on page 50, taken from a small collection of Southern newspapers preserved in the West Sussex Record Office, were quite typical of what was going on at the time.

THE ABOLITION MOVEMENT

To those who saw in America the dream of a new and just society, the existence of slavery was a national sin, the violation of the freedom spelt out in the Declaration of Independence. Although there were Southerners —and even slave-owners like Patrick Henry—who were prepared to avow their guilt, the strength of feeling for abolition within the United States came from the North. Here, after the Revolution, slavery was either abolished outright, as in Vermont, or provisions were made for gradual emancipation as in New York and New Jersey. Since 1831 the campaign had been consistently—and aggressively—waged from Boston by William Lloyd Garrison's newspaper, *The Liberator*. His message was both inflexible and virulent: 'On this subject, I do not wish to think, or speak, or write, with moderation . . . I am in earnest—I will not equivocate —I will not excuse—I will not retreat a single inch—AND I WILL BE HEARD'.[3]

Humanitarian groups, of which in 1836 there were more than five hundred, with a membership by 1840 of over 15,000, took up the cause,

---

[1] Morison & Commager, vol. 1, *op. cit.*, p. 246.
[2] Letter to Lord Lyons, British Ambassador in Washington, from E. Archibald, British Consul in New York, dated Saratoga [Springs, New York State], 3 June 1859. Lyons Papers.
[3] Quoted in Morison & Commager, vol. 1, *op. cit.*, p. 555.

$20 Reward.

RANAWAY from the subscribers on the 16th inst. two negro fellows,

BOB & SAM.

SAM is about 6 feet high, well made, dark colour, about 30 years old, but looks younger; took with him two suits of clothes, a blue linsey homespun janes coat, a pair of mixed janes pantaloons; and other clothing not recollected

BOB is 25 years old, 5 feet 10 inches high, teeth wide apart, dish faced, with a piece bit off one ear, not recollected which, he took with him a green cloth coat, a pair of black cassimer pantaloons, also a pair corded; other clothing not known.

The above reward will be given to any person who will apprehend and lodge these fellows in jail, and inform the subscribers living in Jefferson county East Tennessee, near Mossy creek, so as we get them.

JAMES CAMPBELL,
JAMES REESE.

August 28th 1823 37 70*

Kentucky Reporter
20 October 1823
Cobden Papers 1042.

Thirty Dollars Reward.
Ran-Away

FROM the subscriber on Sunday evening, 3rd inst. a Negro Man named

· **CHARLES,**
AND
A Negro Woman named
PATSEY.

Charles is about twenty-five years of age, five feet nine or ten inches high, slender made, yellow complexion, had on when he went away a blue cloth coat, jeans pantaloons, fur hat considerably worn and rather small. He took with him several articles of clothing not known. Patsey is about twenty-one or two years of age, short, thick set, quite black, coarse features and bad countenance. She had on a white muslin dress and collarette trimmed with black ribbon Took with her two plain domestic cotton dresses, one striped jaconett muslin dress and other articles of clothing not recollected. The above reward will be given for their apprehension, or $15 for either, with all reasonable charges, if delivered to us at the Ætna Furnace, in Hart county, Ky. or secured in any jail in this state so that we can get them again.

HOLDERMAN & WILKINS.

Ætna Furnace, Hart county, Kentucky,
August 4th 1823——3—wp–tf.

Lexington Advertiser & Western
Monitor
(Kentucky)
28 October 1823
Cobden Papers 1042.

Runaway in the Jail of Jefferson County.

COMMITTED to said Jail, a Negro Boy, who says his name is

BILL,

And that he belongs to Thomas B. Reed, of Adams County. The above negro is about 5 feet 6 or 7 inches high, very likely; has a small scar on his right cheek; had on when committed, coarse linen pantaloons and shirt, and a very good fur hat. The said negro having been legally committed by warrant as a runaway, I hereby notify all persons interested, that unless they call for and authenticate their claim to the said negro, within the time prescribed by law, he will be sold for the payment of the prison fees and other charges, agreeably to the act of Assembly in such cases made and provided.

A. JOHNSTON, Jailor J. C.
October 10th, 1823. 76-tf.

The Mississippian & Natchez
Advertiser
15 November 1823
Cobden Papers 1042.

BACON WANTED.

I WISH TO PURCHASE

8000 LBS. GOOD BACON, PRINCIPALL
MIDLINGS.

Lex. March 22d.

WM. PRITCHARTT
68——8t.

Negroes For Sale.

A negro woman, about 20 years of age, a b of about 16, and one of 5 or 6 years of ag are offered for sale for cash. For further inf mation apply at this office

Lex March 23 1824,—68—tf

Lexington Advertiser & Western
Monitor
(Kentucky)
9 April 1824
Cobden Papers 1042.

such as the American Anti-Slavery Society in New York, a cause advanced considerably in 1852 by the publication of Harriet Beecher Stowe's revelations in *Uncle Tom's Cabin*.[1]

i   In November 1864, Major B. Rush Plumly, Chairman of the Board of Education for Freedmen, delivered a long and stirring speech before the 'Free Colored Men of New Orleans' at Economy Hall, New Orleans. A printed copy of the speech, in which he traced the growth of the abolition movement, is preserved in the West Sussex Record Office, some extracts of which are given below.

'In 1787, when the State passed under the Federal Constitution, there were 600,000 slaves in the United States.

In 1830, after nearly half a century of republican national life, the slaves numbered 2,000,000.

Instead of diminishing, as the fathers expected, under the revolutionary pressure of the sentiment of freedom, slavery had strengthened and increased in proportion to our own material progress.

Rooted in the hatred of race, the prejudices of caste and condition, and the love of power, estimated as a money interest at nearly one thousand millions; possessing vast and exclusive political privileges, the system of slavery was the overshadowing and ruling class-interest in the nation. It held the power and dispensed the patronage of the Government . . .

Moulding the Government and public opinion, it reversed the judgment of Washington and Jefferson against itself, and succeeded in establishing a new decision, which declared that slavery was not only the corner-stone of the republican edifice, but that it was ordained of God. With an audacity never exceeded by any organised evil, it assumed to be distinguished by the highest consideration for the colored man it was crushing . . .

Anti-slavery societies sprang up, that demanded its gradual extinction.

The Colonization Society, practically an auxillary of slavery, professed to be looking toward the freedom of the slave.

These associations were little more than safety-valves for the people's innate sense of justice. They did nothing against slavery . . .

There was no danger in postponed emancipation or in any scheme of colonization.

But when the demand came for the immediate and unconditional freedom of the slave, the slaveholder knew that it was the beginning of the end. It was made in no doubtful or halting terms by Mr. William Lloyd Garrison, who in the face of this vast interest demanded its immediate overthrow upon the grounds of humanity and justice.

In the year 1831 . . . [he] established a paper, now the Liberator, in the city of Boston, Massachusetts . . .

. . . in the winter of 1833, the American Anti-Slavery Society was formed with Mr. Garrison as its president. The Society issued a "Declaration of Sentiment", reaffirming the doctrines of the Declaration of Independence on the rights of man . . .

---

[1] Other opinions relating to emancipation are quoted below, pp. 56–59, 66–70, 73–74, 76.

Immediately following the meeting of the society in 1833, measures were taken to build a hall for its uses. The Pennsylvania Hall, a beautiful and commodious building, was erected in Philadelphia. The hall . . . was consecrated . . . to universal freedom.

It was burned down by a furious mob . . . in May, 1837.

Abolitionists, with many colored people, were hunted through peril to places of safety. The colored Orphan Asylum was destroyed over the heads of the helpless inmates. The public journals that defended us were menaced and silenced. The mob was the more violent, because, as they alleged, we were aiming, not only at the freedom of the slave, but at the elevation to equality of the free men of color . . .

Mob succeeded mob. Two years before, in 1835, Mr. Garrison had been led through the streets of Boston, by a mob, with a rope about his neck, to be hung.

Twenty thousand dollars had been offered by a Southern State for his head.

The Abolitionists were not dismayed . . .

Before them were two and a half millions of bondmen and four hundred thousand free people of color; behind them, as they thought, the command of God.

In the convention of 1840, they announced their famous doctrine of "No Union with slaveholders", Mr. Garrison declaring that the American Constitution was, in the language of the Bible, "a covenant with Death and an agreement with Hell", because it sanctioned the enslavement of men.

The Garrisonians declared that no Abolitionist could vote under a constitution that upheld slavery and allowed the degradation of free men of color. On this issue the American Anti-Slavery Society split. Many went off into political parties. The Garrisonians remained a compact body of conscience, intellect, learning, eloquence, poetry, ablaze with enthusiasm, and all alive with moral power . . .

But, increasing in numbers and influence, they redoubled their efforts to arouse the national mind to the great wrong of slavery, by preaching the truth, and by crying aloud for justice to the colored man. The virulence of the pro-slavery parties increased in proportion. Mobs continued . . . They were met by violence in towns and in quiet country places. They were insulted in cars and public conveyances; sneered at in society; despised in churches; hated by politicians, impeded in business; and generally, treated as outlaws and infidels . . .

Still, the Abolitionists continued. They established journals, issued tracts and documents to enlighten the people; sent forth living speakers . . . through every privation and peril. They held fairs and lectures and soirees, flooded Congress and the State Legislatures with petitions, beset politicians with questions, knocked at the doors of the partisan press, hurled the Bible at the clergy, pestered the pro-slavery pulpit until from very torment some sensitive pastor would preach the gospel of freedom.

With skill and secrecy they organised the underground railroad, by which the slave who would indicate his fitness for freedom, by seeking to attain it, might have a chance of escape;[1] or, if arrested, they defended him in courts by all the subtleties of the law and the traditions of the people through the ablest counsel.

Most of the Abolitionists were poor, engaged in some business for their daily bread. It was the practice after their day's labor to go to some town or country place during the long cold evenings of Northern winters, to hold meetings and speak to the people.

We esteemed it no hardship to walk five or six miles over frost and snow, or to drive . . . twice that distance, to and from a meeting for the colored man's rights. In the summer we assembled in the woods, and made the great limbs of the old trees vibrate under our demands for liberty and justice.

Whether speaking publicly or not, we were in constant activity, talking and writing, and vexing and moulding the popular mind. He or she was a poor Abolitionist who could not suffer all things. Each Abolitionist was a pocket-edition of Paul—"ever ready to give a reason for the hope that was in him" . . .

In unshaken faith still laboring on, creating that public sentiment out of which sprang political combinations from the unity of which came the grand party of the Union, on the apex whereof today stands, worthily and triumphant, Abraham Lincoln. Involuntarily the great President is vindicating the Garrisonian Abolitionists in the face of the world, by adopting their most ultra measures, now become, in the providence of God, the means of saving the nation . . .'

Cobden Papers 8, no. 115.

---

[1] The 'underground railroad' was a rescue system for slaves escaping to freedom. By this means escaping slaves were transferred from one abolitionist household to another until safety was reached in the free North or Canada.

The Civil War

Although the Civil War came to be fought on the issue of slavery, it was not in itself the immediate cause. Almost since the birth of the new republic there had been differences of opinion between North and South on sectional issues, differences, which by the mid-19th century were sharpened into a state of 'irrepressible conflict'[1] between two totally different peoples: between an agricultural society rooted in tradition and a slave economy in the South, and in the North an expanding industrial and commercial society well on the way to abolishing slavery altogether.

The immediate cause of the Civil War was political and constitutional, on the issue of whether individual states had the legal right to secede from the Union if they no longer agreed with Union policy.

The actual secession crisis and the first break in the Union was precipitated by the election of Abraham Lincoln as President in 1860. Standing for an anti-slavery policy and measures which would benefit the North and the new Western territories at the expense of the South, it became quite clear that the Union was in mortal danger. 'Nearly every plank in the Republican platform favoured something that the South had fought against for years.'[2] Within weeks of his election, South Carolina adopted its Ordinance of Secession on 20 December declaring that 'the Union now subsisting between South Carolina and the other states under the name of "The United States of America" is hereby dissolved'. Alabama, Florida, Georgia, Louisiana, Mississippi and Texas soon followed the lead, and under Jefferson Davis as president established their own government—the Confederate States of America—under a new constitution and their own flag, the Stars and Bars.

Lincoln's inaugural speech of 4 March 1861 set the seal on war. Although pledging to respect the right to hold slaves in the Southern states, his view of the Union was uncompromising: 'I hold that, in contemplation of universal law and of the Constitution, the Union of these States is perpetual . . . no State upon its own mere motion can lawfully get out of the Union . . . and to the extent of my ability I shall take care, as the Constitution itself expressly enjoins me, that the laws of the Union be faithfully executed in all the States . . .' In six weeks the Civil War had started, with Arkansas, North Carolina, Tennessee and Virginia adding to the Confederacy.

BREAK UP OF A NATION: THE DESPAIR OF AMERICANS

Before the actual outbreak of war in April 1861, many Americans were wrapped in despair and despondency at what was happening to their country. Their republic, which had promised so much, was now threatened with being torn apart. Something of their grief—and shame—is shown in the following two passages.

i   The first is a series of extracts from a speech by Daniel Dougherty, a barrister of Philadelphia, in July 1859. The speech, which was shortly afterwards published under the title of *Fears for the Future of the Republic*,

---

[1] Phrase used by Senator William H. Seward of New York in 1858.
[2] R. B. Nye & J. E. Morpurgo, *A History of the United States: vol. 2: The Growth of the U.S.A.* (1st edn. 1955), p. 456.

compares the achievements and ideals of the past with present threats which he saw might end 'In bloody and exterminating civil war . . .'

'The age in which we live, and the country we call our own, are the most marvellous that have existed since fallen Adam looked his last on Paradise. The boldest flights of the romancer, the wildest dreams of the poet, cannot parallel the rise and progress of this nation.

There are Peers in the British Parliament who are older than this Republic. When Henry Brougham was born[1] the American continent was an almost unbroken wilderness. European kings claimed it as an appendage to their crowns. Here and there might be seen a cultivated spot, the plain yet pleasant home of a thrifty farmer. Occasionally the eye would light on a spacious mansion, where some wealthy gentleman lived in baronial ease.

Lazily sailing up the Hudson or the Delaware, once in a while would come some ship from the Old World. Population was almost exclusively confined to the eastern slopes of the Alleghenies. The missionary, the hunter, and the soldier only had advanced into the valley of the Mississippi; beyond, the land lay in the solemn stillness of primeval nature . . .

Eighty years have sped, and America, touched by the talisman of freedom, has sprung from the downcast mien of neglected provinces into the towering altitude of a colossal empire, whose might the world has never matched, and of which it now doth stand in awe.

The solitude has been broken by the ceaseless din of thirty millions of people, battling for wealth and prosperity . . . Cities founded but yesterday rival in splendor European capitals . . . Our rivers are ever white with the canvas of thousands of ships as they sail and steam to and from the seaports of the world . . .

She has dauntlessly carried her standard amid the Polar seas and over barriers of eternal ice . . . She has annihilated time and space, and . . . made the very elements obey . . .

Such is our country, and such are her achievements.

The solemn question now presents itself and demands an answer from this generation: Is this nation to prosper in the long future as she has in the brief past? . . . Are her glories to depart like a dream? . . .

To insure the stability of our Republican Institutions, and to grasp the rich prizes which hang all along our future, it is not enough that our territory extend from the Atlantic to the Pacific; that population increase; that commerce, manufactures, and agriculture thrive; that arts and education flourish; that science is all powerful. It is essential that the people shall never neglect their political duties, nor be indifferent to the requirements of public virtue, and that they preserve, in all its purity, their system of government . . .

Yet . . . the multitude give no proper attention to their political duties . . .

Thus the vast machinery of this huge Republic . . . is, for the most part, left to the control of bands of men who make politics a trade—men who laugh at integrity—are insensible to patriotism . . .

---

[1] Brougham was born in 1778.

Thus, too, incompetency swaggers in prominent positions, . . . and, with audacious presumption, aspires even to the Presidency! Fraud and corruption hold their revels in high places . . . Discord rears her horrid front, and a division of the Union is gloried in by those who have sworn to defend the Constitution . . .

. . . The Revolution, its trials and its triumphs, are forgotten. The Constitution . . . is pronounced a failure. The Union . . . is declared by them to have outlived its purposes. They are bent on creating jealousies among the people, engendering sectional hate, and enkindling the fires of fierce civil war . . .

In the North, conventions composed of delegates representing distant constituencies, outrage all propriety by the violence of their fanatical appeals, and devise means to oppose the execution of national laws.

In the South, conventions of able men advocate the opening of the slave trade, . . . and with defiant tone, proclaim treason to the Republic.

Unchecked, where will all this end? In bloody and exterminating civil war—in the separation of the South from the North—in the downfall of the Republic—in the destruction of liberty . . .'

Lyons Papers.

ii   C. C. Felton, President of Harvard, was equally grieved by the state of the nation. As secession fever gripped the South, and just five days before South Carolina's Ordinance of Secession, he wrote to his friend Lord Lyons[1] in Washington on 15 December 1860.

'. . . What a spectacle you are witnessing at Washington. I see no hope for my distracted country. We seem destined to break up into a cluster of warring republics—a misery to ourselves and an object of contempt to the world. We are rushing headlong upon a terrible catastrophe— folly of speech and madness of mind driving us to perdition. I am not wholly unprepared for this result. Last winter I heard nothing in the Congress, but mutual accusation; no statesmanship, no greatness of mind; nothing but wretched repetitions of newspaper slang and violence, and in social life, nothing but exasperation and hate between South and North . . . My God! I seem to have no country . . . I shall belong to the last generation of United Americans, and you may be the last British minister to the United States.'

Lyons Papers.

THE DIVIDED NORTH

The North in itself was as divided as the nation as a whole when it came to the leading issues of the day. Lincoln himself was only a minority President, supported by 40 per cent of the popular vote. There were many Northerners who wanted the South to secede in peace; others who wanted concessions on slavery for the South. And between the extremists on both sides there were large areas of agreement and genuine sympathies. Many of Lincoln's own party were appalled at his inflexibility. He was

---

[1] Richard Bickerton Pemell Lyons, 2nd Baron and 1st Earl Lyons (1817–1887), British Ambassador to the United States, 1858–1865. He was related to the Duke of Norfolk of Arundel Castle, Sussex. His American (and other diplomatic and personal) papers were preserved at Arundel Castle until transferred to the West Sussex Record Office in 1975. A catalogue is in preparation (1976).

inept and awkward, a political nonentity, a 'Simple Susan', an 'Ape' or a 'Baboon'. To S. Austin Allibone of Philadelphia 'We are now cursed by an imbecile, or a traitor, in the person of the President of the United States . . .'[1]

i   '. . . two millions seven hundred thousand voters do not want to interfere with Slavery.'

Letter to Lord Lyons from Delphy Carlin, Brooklyn, New York, 2 December 1861.

'. . . This is an unnatural war, accidental I would say, for out of three millions votes of the North, there are only three hundred thousand abolitionist. So it is that two millions seven hundred thousand voters do not want to interfere with Slavery. Your Lordship will perceive that the South has been grossly deceived as to the intention of a great majority of the people of the North. It would seem that the three hundred thousand abolitionist have a powerful influence, for they nearly rule over the two millions seven hundred thousand voters, I mean in elections . . .

Your Lordship will percive that the North is willing to grant everything reasonable which the South could ask, even an amendment to the Constitution, to better define the word Servitude. Slavery in this country will disapear soon enough if we Americans have the common sense not to destroy entirely the country. The only substitute for Slave labour in this country South, will be the Chinian, their labour will be cheaper than that of Slave labour. Slavery will become more & more repugnant to man, and this country must look forward to gradual emancipation . . .'

Lyons Papers.

ii   The Plight over Slavery.

Amidst mounting concern for the state of the nation, a packed Union meeting was held in Faneuil Hall, Boston, on 8 December 1859. A printed 'phonographic report' made by the *Boston Courier* is amongst the Lyons Papers in the West Sussex Record Office. One of the principal speakers, the Hon. Edward Everett, whilst sympathetic to the slaves, believed there should be as much sympathy for the slave-owners themselves who were caught up in a very difficult situation. Besides, immediate and wholesale emancipation would pose serious threats to the stability of the North.

'. . . Sir, I have on three or four different occasions . . . visited all the Southern and Southwestern States, with the exception of Arkansas and Alabama. I have enjoyed the hospitality of the city and the country . . . I have been admitted to the confidence of the domestic circle, and I have seen there touching manifestations of the kindest feelings, by which that circle, in all its members, high and low, master and servant, can be bound together; and when I contemplate the horrors that would have ensued had the tragedy on which the curtain rose at Harper's Ferry been acted out, through all its scenes of fire and sword, of lust and murder, of rapine and desolation, to the final catastrophe, I am filled with emotions to which no words can do

---

[1] Letter to Lord Lyons, 12 February 1861. Lyons Papers.

justice.[1] There could of course be but one result, and that well deserving the thoughtful meditation of those . . . who think that the welfare of the colored race could by any possibility be promoted by the success of such a movement . . . The white population of the Southern States alone . . . outnumbers the colored race in the ratio of two to one: in the Union at large in the ratio of seven to one; and if (which Heaven avert) they should be brought into conflict, it could end only in the extermination of the latter . . .

Such being the case, some one may ask why does not the South fortify herself against the possible occurence of such a catastrophe, by doing away with the one great source from which alone it can spring? This is a question easily asked, and I am not aware that it is our duty at the North to answer it; but it may be observed that great and radical changes in the framework of Society . . . will not wait on the bidding of an impatient philanthropy. They can only be brought about in the lapse of time . . . have those, who rebuke the South for the continuance of slavery, considered that neither the present generation nor the preceding one is responsible for its existence? The African slave trade was prohibited by Act of Congress fifty-one years ago, and many years earlier by the separate Southern States. The entire colored population, with the exception, perhaps, of a few hundreds surreptitiously introduced,[2] is native to the soil. Their ancestors were conveyed from Africa in the ships of Old England and New England. They now number between three and four millions. Has any person . . . proposed, in sober earnest, a practical method of wholesale emancipation? . . . has any person, whose opinion is entitled to the slightest respect, ever undertaken to sketch out the details of a plan for effecting the change at once, by any legislative measure that could be adopted? Consider only, I pray you, that it would be to ask the South to give up one thousand millions of property, which she holds by a title satisfactory to herself, as the first step. Then estimate the cost of an adequate outfit for the self support of the emancipated millions; then reflect on the derangement of the entire industrial system of the South, and all the branches of commerce and manufactures that depend on its great staples; then the necessity of conferring equal political privileges on the emancipated race, who being free would be content with nothing less . . . then the consequent organization of two great political parties on the basis of color, and the eternal feud which would rage between them; and finally the overthrow into the free States of a vast multitude of needy and helpless emigrants . . . Should *we*, sir, with all our sympathy for the colored race (and I do sincerely sympathize with them . . .), give a very cordial reception to two or three hundred thousand destitute emancipated slaves? Does not every candid man see, that every one of these steps presents difficulties of the most formidable character—difficulties for which, as far as I know, no man and no party has proposed a solution. And is it, sir, for the attainment of

[1] John Brown, a fanatical abolitionist, attempted to raise a slaves' revolt. On 16 October 1859, with a band of eighteen supporters, he attacked Harper's Ferry, Virginia, killed the mayor, took prisoners and seized the Federal arsenal. Followers went to rouse the slaves, but without success, and the revolt failed. Brown was hanged on 2 December 1859, six days before this public meeting at Boston.

[2] But note the findings of the British Consul in New York in the same year. See above, p. 49.

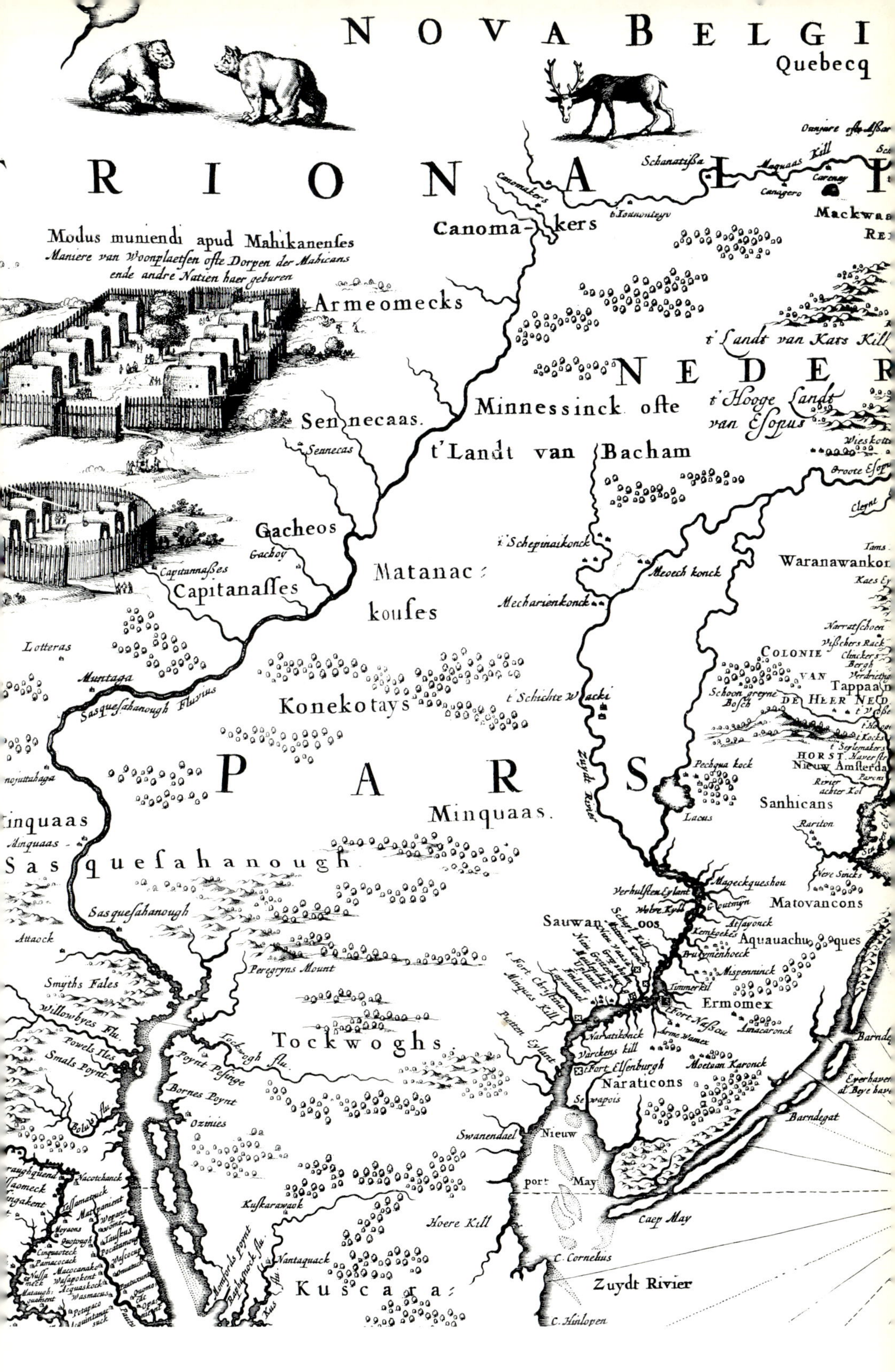

Plate No. I

Section of North American map by Nicolas Visscher, undated, but published between 1638 and 1664
(see pages 2–3)

Cape May, New Jersey, is bottom right; Fort Nassau is the site of Gloucester, New Jersey, and Fort
Christina the site of Wilmington, Delaware

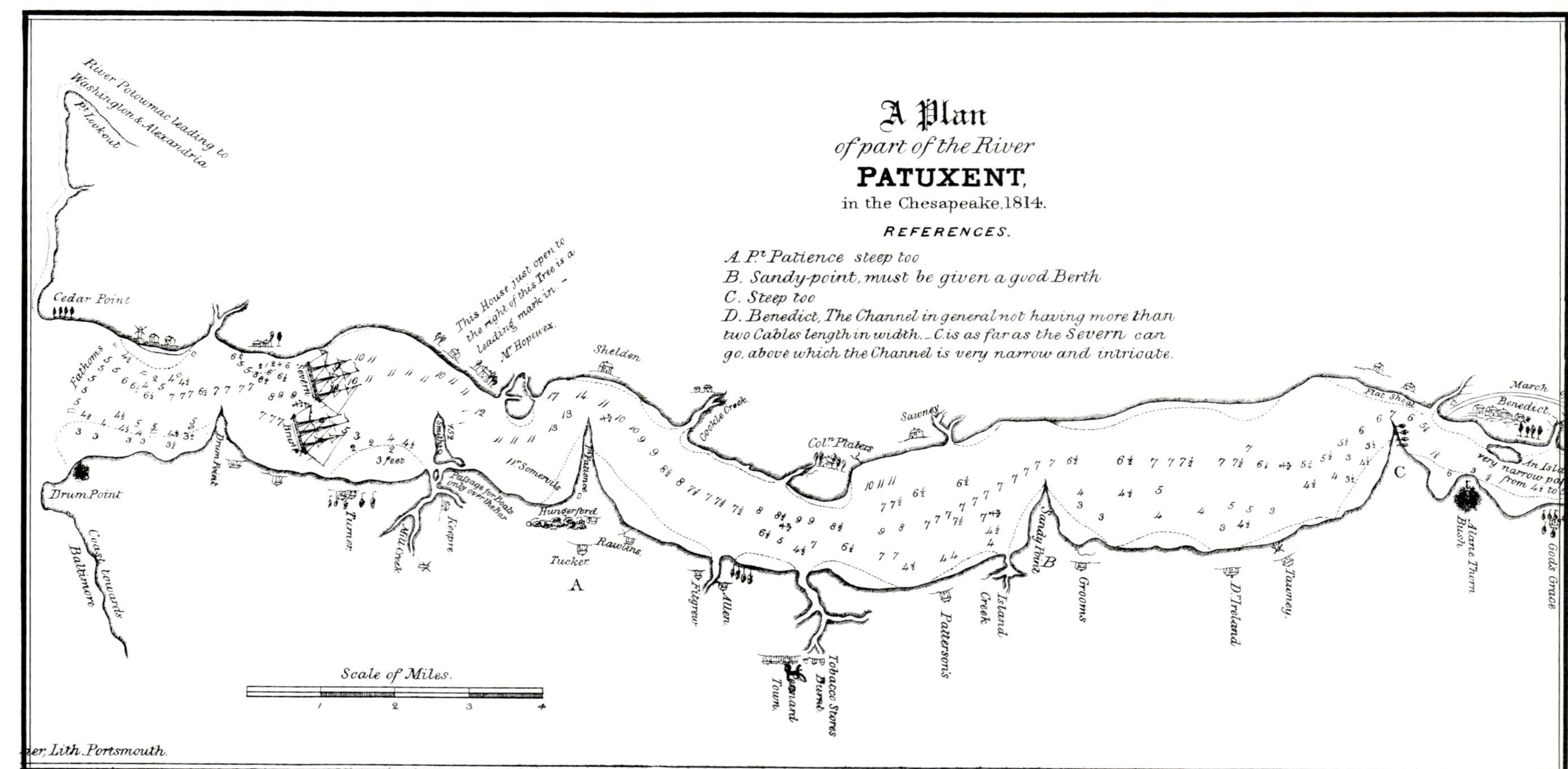

Part of plan of the River Patuxent showing the route of the British naval operation, August 1814

Troops were landed at Benedict from where they marched to attack Washington. The beginning of this route march is indicated between the words 'March' and 'Benedict' on the extreme right of the plan

FARMERS, MECHANICS, AND LABOURERS,

WHO ARE DESIROUS TO

EMIGRATE to the UNITED STATES

Are informed that an English Colony has been formed in the

COUNTIES OF MERCER, WYOMING, AND TAZEWELL,

In Western Virginia,

AND THAT ARRANGEMENTS HAVE BEEN ENTERED INTO TO DESPATCH

FROM LIVERPOOL

EARLY IN THE MONTH OF MARCH NEXT,

THE FINE FAST-SAILING FIRST-CLASS SHIP,

SUTLEJ,

A 1 at Lloyd's.   DIRECT   **659 Tons Register.**

To City Point, near Richmond, Virginia.

This superb Ship has a most excellent Cabin, an unusually spacious Poop, and superior Accommodations for Intermediate and Steerage Passengers; it is recommended that Parties availing themselves of this opportunity to proceed should meet together, as often as practicable, for the purpose of acquaintance, and for arranging plans for promoting their interests on arrival.

WESTERN VIRGINIA is now in a most successful and prosperous condition, and offers advantages which are not to be surpassed in any of the States. The Settlers who have already proceeded there, without any exception, express themselves highly satisfied with the healthful nature of the Climate, and the fertility of the Lands.

NEITHER DEPOSITS NOR CONTRACTS

Are required from Emigrants to Purchase Land.

After arrival in the Colony, and examining for themselves, they are at perfect liberty to select such Tracts of Land as they may consider most advantageous to their own interests.

Pamphlets forwarded on Receipt of Four Stamps, fully descriptive of the Colony, the Climate, Quality of the Soil, Productions, its Local advantages, and other needful and interesting Information.

For further Particulars, apply to **ROBERT C. GIST, Esq.,** 8, St. Martin's Place, Trafalgar Square; to **E. JONES,** 45, Union Street, Liverpool; or to

WILLIAMS & FORD,

26, BIRCHIN LANE, LONDON.

Emigration Poster, *c.* 1850

(See page 39)

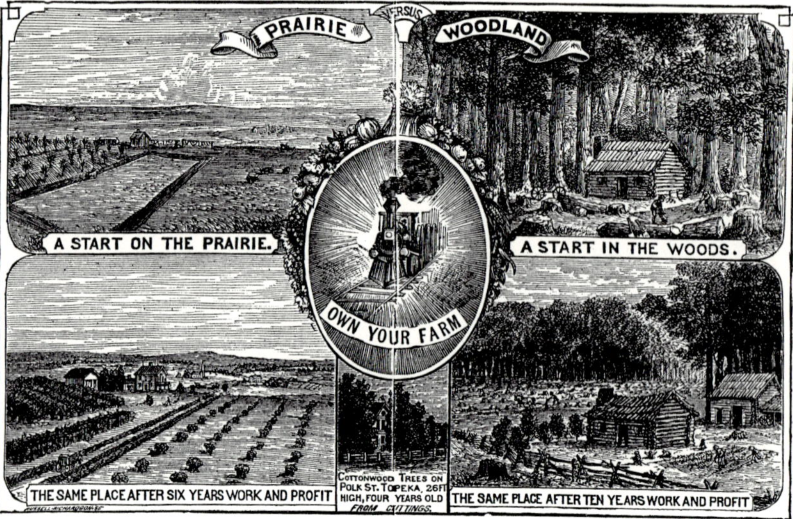

Cover of leaflet advertising emigration to Kansas, *c.* 1880

(See pages 45–47)

objects so manifestly impracticable, pursued too, by the bloody pathways of treason and murder, that we will allow the stupendous evil which now threatens us, to come upon the country? Shall we permit this curiously compacted body politic, the nicest adjustment of human wisdom, to go to pieces? . . .'

Lyons Papers.

iii   'Neither the Constitution nor the laws of the United States can be tortured into conferring the war-making power upon the President . . .'

Although the State of Maryland joined the North in the Civil War as one of the border slave states, its people shared much in common with Southern traditions and attitudes. There was, therefore, sharp reaction in Maryland to Lincoln's Proclamation of 15 April 1861 summoning seventy-five thousand volunteers to crush combinations 'too powerful to be suppressed by the ordinary course of judicial proceedings'. It was seen as a summons tantamount to making war on friendly sister states, 'a declaration of war against the Southern Confederacy— . . . a deliberate summons to . . . shed each other's blood, in wantoness and hate' according to the Maryland Committee on Federal Relations.

Any fears that Maryland might secede and join the Confederacy, however, were finally quashed when Federal troops took Baltimore on 13 May 1861, just four days after the Committee's fiercely pro-Southern report had been presented to the House of Delegates.

Report of the Maryland Committee on Federal Relations, May 1861.

'. . . The President of the United States, by his Proclamation of the 15th of April, had called upon a portion of the States to place at his disposal a body of militia, to the number of seventy-five thousand men. The Proclamation was directed against the people of the newly-formed Southern Confederacy, and its purposes and policy were obvious, although its terms were technically shaped in conformity with the Act of Congress of 1795. It recited . . . in the language of the Act, "that the laws of the United States were opposed, and the execution thereof was obstructed", in the seven seceded States, "by combinations too powerful to be suppressed by the ordinary course of judicial proceedings, or by the powers vested in the Marshals", and it called forth the militia of the other States . . . "to suppress such combinations, and to cause the laws to be duly executed" . . .

. . . [His Proclamation] kindled so intense a flame of resentment and resistance. His proclamation was regarded as a declaration of war against the Southern Confederacy—as a deliberate summons to the people of the two sections, into which his party and its principles had so hopelessly divided the land, to shed each other's blood, in wantoness and hate. A scheme so full of wickedness—so utterly subversive of every principle upon which our government was founded, and so sure to involve the destruction of that government . . . The people of the seceded States, whether constitutionally or unconstitutionally, had separated themselves from this government and established a federal government of their own, with all the forms of a constitution and all the substantial attributes of actual independence . . .

Neither the Constitution nor the laws of the United States can be tortured into conferring the war-making power upon the President in any contigency. Where foreign nations are concerned, the plain language of the fundamental law entrusts it to Congress only. As against the States of the Union, the possibility of such a thing is not even contemplated, much less provided for. Like parricide at Athens, it was held too heinous and impossible, to be named, even for the purpose of punishment . . .

But, illegal and unconstitutional as was the war which the Proclamation summoned one section of the country against the other, the causes and purposes of that war, made it chiefly obnoxious to the people of Maryland and of the Slave States of the Border.[1] It was a war of propagandism and of sectional aggression and domination. It was a war of the North upon the South. It was a war in which the dominant section had seized upon the name and flag, and resources and powers, of the General Government, and was abusing them for its own ends, and for the permanent establishment of its dominion over the other section . . . It was a war waged against a people of our own name and blood; who sought peace and kindly relations with us, and who asked only to be let alone and to be permitted to govern themselves. It could bring no good, for it could end only in the defeat of the invaders or the subjugation of the invaded, and in either case the Union, which our fathers left to us, must be at an end. Subjugated provinces could not be sister States . . . The South had entrenched itself upon the principle of self-government. It had offered to negotiate . . . upon all matters of common property and divided interest, claiming only that three millions of people had a right to throw off a Government, by which they no longer desired to be ruled, and to live under another Government of their own choosing. Unless the American Revolution was a crime, the declaration of American Independence a falsehood, and every patriot and hero of 1776 a traitor, the South was right and the North was wrong . . . The people of Maryland, therefore, could have but one choice in such a contest, and while as devoted to the Union and as loyal to the Constitution, as the people of any of the thirteen States, who had formed the one and pledged themselves to the other, they could not but throw the whole weight of their sympathies upon that side to which common interests and institutions inclined them, and with which they felt that the right and the truth were. Nor was it a matter of sympathy merely. The breach of the Constitution involved in the coercive policy of the Administration, was a breach of their rights, and no less than an unlawful aggression upon the rights of the Southern people. It was an overthrow of the principles of free government, and could end in nothing but an ignominious annihilation of the noble institutions of the Republic . . .

. . . Maryland . . . is treated as a conquered enemy. Her soil is occupied; her property and that of her citizens are sequestered; her public highways are seized and obstructed; her laws are suspended; her capital is converted into a military post; her Legislature is compelled, in the language of her Executive, to consult its "safety" by holding its sessions at a distance from her offices and archives; troops are quartered around the peaceful homesteads of her people; her citizens are subjected to the illegal and arbitary violence of military arrest and confinement; her very freedom . . . is under the armed heel of the Government . . .

---

[1] The Slave States of the Border were Delaware, Kansas, Maryland and Missouri.

The State of Maryland is under military rule. Partly for military convenience, and partly for chastisement, her free institutions have been temporarily suspended by the War Department, and her name blotted out . . . from the list of free governments . . .

Finally, the Committee respectfully submit to the House the following resolutions . . .

. . . That the State of Maryland owes it to her own self-respect and her respect for the Constitution, not less than to her deepest and most honorable sympathies, to register this her solemn protest against the war which the Federal Government has declared upon the Confederate States of the South, and our sister and neighbor Virginia, and to announce her resolute determination to have no part or lot, directly or indirectly, in its prosecution.

. . . That the State of Maryland earnestly and anxiously desires the restoration of peace between the belligerent sections of the country, and the President, authorities, and people of the Confederate States, having, over and over again . . . declared that they seek only peace and self-defence, and to be let alone, and that they are willing to throw down the sword, the instant that the sword now drawn against them shall be sheathed, the Senators and Delegates of Maryland do beseech and implore the President of the United States to accept the olive branch which is thus held out to him . . .

. . . That the State of Maryland desires the peaceful and immediate recognition of the independence of the Confederate States . . .

. . . That the present military occupation of Maryland, being . . . in flagrant violation of the Constitution, the General Assembly of the State, in the name of her people, does hereby protest against the same, and against the oppressive restrictions and illegalities with which it is attended; calling upon all good citizens . . . to abstain from all violent and unlawful interference . . . with the troops in transit through our territory or quartered amongst us . . .'

Lyons Papers.

CHARLESTON, SOUTH CAROLINA:
CENTRE OF SOUTHERN EXTREMISM

A year before South Carolina took the lead in seceding from the Union in December 1860, the flames of mass hysteria were sweeping the people in a frenzy of hate against the North. Fanned by the recent news of John Brown's abortive attempt to raise a slaves' rebellion at Harper's Ferry, the atmosphere was tense. The extremist centre was Charleston, and it was from here that in December 1859 the British Consul, Robert Bunch, reported to the British Ambassador in Washington, Lord Lyons, on the state of local feeling. His letters give a vivid glimpse of the tensions that were to work themselves into secession by the end of the following year.

i   Charleston, 3 December 1859.

'. . . The state of excitement here is really intense. A dissolution of the Union is advocated by everybody—but what can one State do? In the meantime *this* Commonwealth is instituting "Vigilance Committees" in every village—turning people away, sometimes with and sometimes without a travelling wrapper of tar & feathers—opening letters in the

Post Office, and conducting itself in a truly Republican manner, by guaranteeing to everyone absolute freedom of thought and speech—provided the conclusion and language happened to be very much in favour of slavery . . .'

Lyons Papers.

ii   Charleston, 7 December 1859.

'. . . I beg to thank your Lordship for your telegram of yesterday, respecting the arrival of Disph. no. 16. In these ticklish times Post Offices are not too safe, and if the excitement into which people about here are working themselves should increase in intensity, cyphering will be our only refuge . . .

I have lately had a visit from a very intelligent young Englishman who has been employed for six years by a large Boston House (Chase Brothers & Co.) to travel for them in the South. He wished me to give him a British Passport, which I did, and further assured him that so long as he conformed to the laws, and abstained from meddling in political questions, I would protect him, at every hazard, in my Consular District. He told me that the tyranny of the Vigilance Committees was beyond exaggeration. That he *had seen* a letter which he wrote to his wife taken out of the Post Office, opened and read before his face. That he *had seen* a man whom he knew to be a respectable merchant, head of a house, in Boston, stripped and flogged at Raleigh, N.C., for being suspected of being an abolitionist. That he had himself been searched two or three times and threatened with lynching, & that all the Northern men were rapidly leaving the South for fear of their lives. I leave your Lordship to judge whether or no such conduct will tend to heal the breach between North & South.

Of course, as these "emissaries" from the North come . . . to collect the money due for the thousand articles of common use which the South cannot make for itself, it is a capital dodge to avoid payment of the bills by raising the cry of "abolitionism" against the collector . . .'

Lyons Papers.

iii   Charleston, 10 December 1859.

'. . . Now, scarcely a voice is raised in favor of the Union—everybody . . . is in favor of immediate separation if the South fails to secure from the present Congress more effectual guarantees, not only against attacks à la John Brown (what a name for a hero! how could it be got into an Epic?) but against any interference at all with slavery on the part of the Free States. I think, therefore, that I can safely assure your Lordship that the feeling against the Union, *just now*, is stronger and more widely spread than it has ever been before . . .

. . . A great Republic like this—the evolution of a great thought—of any great experiment, is not to be broken to pieces by one, or half a dozen blows. It has immense vitality and will, in my humble judgement, stand a good deal more knocking about than it has yet had. Besides which, are the South prepared to organise a government which shall take its place? Why, I do not believe that any three Southern States could be found to agree upon any one single point, except perhaps that every man has an inalienable right to "wallop his own nigger"—a truth, which however valuable or incontestable, will scarcely suffice for the building of an Empire.

62

My own belief is that we shall see, before long, a reaction at the North. There is, as your Lordship will have seen, a substratum of conservative common sense at the bottom of the American character which altho' covered and concealed by the fantastic folly of the masses, still exists to be counted upon when the need arises. So soon as that is dug down to— in other words, so soon as people are really persuaded that the Union is in danger, we shall see a great change. The ultraists on both sides [of] the Potomac will be rejected by their constituents, and compromise will be the order of the day. Of course, one cannot go on compromising for ever, but the doom will be averted for a time.

Small as is my sympathy with Democracy (for I hate it as I do sour claret) I own to a sneaking kindness for our American off-shoot, and I should see with regret the application of the pruning-knife. Full of faults as the system is, it has . . . at any rate not interfered with the performance of great works, and it has much to do yet for the good of mankind. Once divided, the prestige is gone. The principle once admitted, where will the practice stop? . . .'

Lyons Papers.

iv   Charleston, 18 December 1859.

'. . . I continue to receive accounts from travellers in the Southern States of the systematic annoyance which is inflicted upon them at every Rail Road station and in every Town which lies in their route, if by their appearance or manner they are suspected of belonging to the Northern Country or to England. In the vast majority of instances the annoyance simply takes the form of a close examination into the motives which the travellers may have for visiting the South, their pursuits, residences and acquaintances; in rarer cases the verbal "search" is accompanied by investigation of letters and pocket books . . .

This morning I have received an interesting visit from a Canadian physician, Dr. Alexander Milton Ross, who is on his way to New Orleans. He tells me that he has himself been interrogated upon several occasions between Richmond and Charleston, and that in Wilmington he was told that "if he was an Englishman he must be Abolitionist". It is, however, fair to presume that the establishment of the former fact saved him from the ill consequences which would have attended, under other circumstances, their interrogators conviction of the latter, as he was not molested. He travelled, however, with an unfortunate Bostonian who had made himself "obnoxious", and who had one half of his head & one whisker shaved off, and his entire face burnt and blackened with Nitrate of silver . . .'

Lyons Papers.

FORT SUMTER: FIRST SHOTS OF THE CIVIL WAR

One of the first tasks to face the Confederate States on their secession from the Union was the occupation of Federal property. Post offices and other official buildings such as customs houses and military installations were taken over with little incident. But Fort Sumter, a Federal offshore garrison commanding Charleston Harbour, was a different matter. The Federal government refused to surrender. On 10 April General Beauregard, commander of Confederate troops at Charleston, issued an ultimatum: evacuation and surrender, or the Fort would be destroyed by his shore batteries. The garrison commander, Major Anderson, refused to surrender, and so in the early hours of 12 April the first guns of the Civil War were fired. With the Fort destroyed after continual pounding for more than a day, Anderson surrendered.

The bombardment provided a magnificent—almost theatrical—spectacle to the people of Charleston as they watched the duel from every vantage point amongst the rooftops and along the harbour. One of the spectators was Robert Bunch, the British Consul who wrote the letters already quoted above. His further letters to Lord Lyons in Washington record the scene.

i   Charleston, 5 April 1861.

'. . . Fort Sumter hangs in the balance, but we are promised action of some sort in a few days. As to reinforcing being impossible, it is utter nonsence . . . I am quite satisfied that 200 men in boats, with barrels of pemmican & concentrated food of various kinds could cross in any dark night . . .'

Lyons Papers.

ii   Charleston, 9 April 1861.

'. . . We are in the most frightful state of commotion imaginable. It is fully believed that the U.S. Govt. intend to reinforce Fort Sumter, and every man is under arms. If the news from Washn. be true that reinforcements are on their way, there will be a desperate fight here before we are many days, perhaps hours, older . . .

. . . Goodness only knows what is before us. It is just possible that the faithful & attendant peasantry may take advantage of everybody being away fighting the Fort to start a little private war now on their own account in the city. I have been looking at the halyards of my flagstaff to see whether they want renewing, as the Union Jack will probably go up en permanence . . .'

Lyons Papers.

iii   Charleston, 11 April 1861.

'Fort Sumter is perfectly surrounded by men. There are certainly between 6 and 700 on the various Islands. My fear is that even if the U.S. supplies & reinforcements do not arrive, an attack will be made by the Southern troops . . .

Everything is upside now and cannot continue long in this state . . .'

Lyons Papers.

iv   Charleston, 13 April 1861.

'. . . The garrison of Fort Sumter was recommended to surrender, unconditionally (as we hear) on Thursday night. Major Anderson, having declined to comply with the request, the various Batteries opened on him at $\frac{1}{4}$ to 5 on Friday morning. The attacking Batteries are eight in number, five at least of them firing shell. Major Anderson has no shell and from the small number of his men can only work four guns. Consequently not a single man has been hurt on the S.C. side. As the bombardment lasted about 15 hours yesterday, your Lordship can judge by this fact what enormous risk the seceders have run. There has literally not been a scratch inflicted on one of them.

The Almighty having been pleased to deprive me altogether of intelligence and senses, I yesterday went in a row boat . . . down the harbour to take a look at matters and things . . . I had a capital view of the firing on both sides, but do not think that what I saw was sufficient to repay me for my trouble.

Today, the firing which was kept up at intervals during the night, has been renewed with increased vigour. At 8 a.m. Fort Sumter was badly on fire, blazing merrily. In about 45 minutes the conflagration abated. Subsequently, however, there have been two explosions in the Fort, one of which I saw. It looked very badly, but it is impossible to say what the damage has been. Anderson is evidently suffering today . . . I do not think that Anderson can hold out much longer unless he be reinforced. The odds are too great against him.

I send an account from the Charleston Paper . . .[1]

wdai   katac   xrad   mbzc
anns   diut   agdm.   [2]

2.30 p.m.

About an hour ago Fort Sumter's flagstaff was shot away. It remained down some time but at last the flag appeared, seemingly hoisted on a chimney. In about 20 minutes, however, it came down and a white flag was run up in its place. So we suppose Anderson has surrendered, but no particulars are known as yet. Of course there is frightful excitement, and, equally of course, it is now quite evident that the Almighty is on our side. Also that our cause is a just and holy one.[3]

6.30 p.m.

The Fort has surrendered unconditionally I believe. So far as I can learn not one soul has been hurt on either side, which after 33 hours bombarding is a little curious. But we live in curious times . . .'

Lyons Papers.

RICHARD COBDEN AND THE CIVIL WAR

The English politician Richard Cobden felt an intense and deep admiration for America. He had savoured it at first hand in 1835 and 1859,[4] was overwhelmed with its physical grandeur and material prosperity, had invested heavily in the Illinois Central Rail Road,[5] and made a great many friends. The whole American way of life and its achievements

---

[1] Enclosed with this letter is a cutting from a Charleston newspaper announcing the commencement of hostilities.

[2] It has not been possible to decypher this coded message. Although Bunch refers to sending a suggested cyphering system to Lord Lyons (letter, 7 December 1859) using 'the letters of the Alphabet shuffled about' this has not been found in the Lyons Papers. Note, however, that there is a key to a cypher system with the correspondence from the British Consul at Richmond, F. J. Cridland.
This letter with this coded message from Bunch was probably intercepted and opened by the Southern postal authorities. Immediately above the coded message is written in pencil 'a pack of horrid lies'.

[3] Sentiments not to be taken literally. Bunch might have written in this way to suggest sympathy with the South should the letter be opened by Southern agents. When writing to Lord Lyons on another occasion (19 April 1861) he writes 'We talk of going Northwards & ejecting the present occupant of the White House'.

[4] For extracts from his American journals see below, pp. 77–90.

[5] There are some official papers relating to the Illinois Central Rail Road Company in Cobden Papers 396 and 398. There is also a series of letters from W. H. Osborn, the railroad promoter and President of this Company, to Cobden. See Francis W. Steer (ed.), *The Cobden Papers* (1964).

—except for the stain of slavery—were for Cobden a matter of profound satisfaction and exhilaration.

At seeing America about to be torn apart by war he was doubly grieved. It was the country he loved and respected, but above all he was a man of peace, dedicated to the cause of international peace and understanding. He could not remain unmoved. To Cobden this meant doing something positive to help resolve some of the differences between North and South, and his efforts for peace, through speeches, writings and letters, won the admiration of moderate, peace-loving America.

The conflict between North and South drew Cobden in yet further when its repercussions seemed likely to bring war between the North and Great Britain. The Northern blockade of Southern ports, cutting off raw cotton from Britain and threatening ruin to Lancashire, then the provocation of the *Trent* and *Alabama* incidents,[1] brought both countries perilously close to the edge of yet another Anglo-American war. With his friend and political ally John Bright, Cobden urged moderation. Through a voluminous behind-the-scenes correspondence[2] he was in direct contact with many of the leading men of the day on both sides of the Atlantic; he had little faith in the formal diplomatic channels, fearing that the British government's bluntness and Lord Lyons' inexperience as Ambassador in Washington had all the makings of a dangerous situation.[3] He interceded between Lord John Russell, British Foreign Secretary, and Charles Sumner, Chairman of the American Senate Foreign Relations Committee. To Sumner he relayed the moods of the British people and government.[4] Ever putting international co-operation before national prejudice he wrote to Sumner that he could 'now best serve the interests of humanity by telling you frankly the state & progress of opinion here'.[5] Sumner often passed Cobden's letters direct to Lincoln. 'From their [Cobden's and Bright's] unofficial position they were able to ease tensions and resolve misunderstandings in a manner not open to Palmerston or Russell as Prime Minister and Foreign Secretary.' Over the *Trent* issue 'their advice may . . . have been crucial'.[6]

On the issue of slavery Cobden was quite clear. It was 'a curse';[7] he believed the Southerners—'an aristocracy in *the saddle* (riding the black man)'[7]—would eventually be forced to free the slaves without a war. For

---

[1] Both incidents resulted in a diplomatic crisis. In November 1861 the British mail packet *Trent* was intercepted by a Northern warship and two Southern envoys on their way to Europe were taken prisoner. In July 1862 the British built, and largely British-manned, Southern warship *Alabama* slipped out of the Mersey against—it was alleged—the wishes of the British government. The *Alabama* created havoc amongst Northern shipping. (See the pamphlet *English Neutrality. Is the Alabama a British Pirate?* (New York, 1863); Cobden Papers 244.)

[2] The letters *from* Cobden in this section are taken from *copies* in the West Sussex Record Office. Where possible these copies have been checked against the originals amongst the Cobden material in the British Museum.

[3] 'I have no faith in Lord Lyons in his present delicate position. He ought to have been a man of mature judgment and large experience instead of a Lord without any antecedents.' Cobden to Bright, 1 November 1861. Cobden Papers 45. For the original letter see British Museum, Add. MS. 43,651, f. 281.

[4] For references to the correspondence between Cobden and Sumner in the West Sussex Record Office see *The Cobden Papers, op. cit.* According to a note amongst the Cobden letters in the British Museum there are thirty-six original letters from Cobden to Sumner at Harvard University. British Museum, Add. MS. 43,678, f. 76.

[5] 11 July 1862. Cobden Papers 114, p. 54.

[6] Donald Read, *Cobden and Bright: A Victorian Political Partnership* (1967), pp. 222, 223.

[7] Quoted from letters to Samuel Lucas, 3 October 1863 and 5 November 1862 respectively. Cobden Papers 135.

all his hatred of slavery he hated the violence of warfare even more and would have 'preferred to see the black man emancipated in any other way than by the sword'.[1] The weakness its existence gave to Southern society would be its downfall, for he saw 'the inherent weakness of a Slave owning community whose social organisation dissolves when brought into contact with a higher civilization. It is the feudalism of the 13th century contending against the freedom of intelligence of New England.'[2]

Cobden was born and lived at Heyshott, near Midhurst in Sussex. Many of his personal and political papers have been deposited in the West Sussex Record Office. From the Cobden Papers a small selection of letters relating to the Civil War has been made: firstly a series written by Cobden himself, and secondly a series sent to Cobden by both American and English writers.

i Letter from Richard Cobden, Midhurst, to Thomas B. Potter, M.P., Buile Hill, Manchester, 1 November 1861.

'. . . The state of things in America is so astounding that although I have had pretty good opportunities of knowing that country, I am at a loss what is to be the issue. I am, however, strongly of opinion that the issue of *separation*, at an early period, which is generally awaited by our leading men in England, is not going to happen till after the struggle has been protracted for a long time & assumed quite a new character. There are geographical obstacles which render separation almost impossible. I am quite sure that the Great West will not permanently submit to see the Lower Mississippi in the hands of a foreign power. The Mississippi Valley will one day contain 200 millions of free men, the richest population perhaps in the world. There is nearly 1000 miles square of the finest land in the world. Egypt & Mesopotamia are mere garden plots in comparison. Watered with 20,000 miles of navigable streams & lakes, & possessing beneath the surface perhaps ten times as much coal as in all Europe, this great region will never succumb permanently to the comparitively weak & uncivilised population of the states of Mississippi, Louisiana, & Arkansas which occupies the lower part of that great river, which serves as the sole navigable outlet to the Gulf of Mexico for all the Upper region. If I were to bet upon the issue it would be in favour of a compromise, if Europe does not interfere. But North & South can never live happily together again. They must be unhappy for a time & then something else will happen . . .'

Cobden Papers 38.

ii Letter from Richard Cobden, London, to W. H. Osborn, New York, 23 May 1862.

'. . . Without presuming to know what may be the state of opinion in the North or South, or what prospect there may be of peace, I conclude that there must be a great desire on both sides to put an end to the war, if possible . . . But to restore the Union by force, and to hold it by force only, is quite inconsistent with the maintenance of a Republic. The only alternative then between a permanent state of military violence and a voluntary separation is such a basis for reuniting North and South as shall be satisfactory to both sides. For this end, mutual concession is an indispensible condition. Especially is it necessary that the

---

[1] Letter to John Cassell, the publisher, 11 January 1863. Cobden Papers 54, p. 29. For further extracts from this letter see below, pp. 68–69.
[2] In letter to Thomas B. Potter, M.P., 21 August 1864. Cobden Papers 39.

party which has been unsuccessful in arms should be conciliated. This the North can afford to do, and in fact, magnanimity in victory is the duty of the victors. If the South have any grievance, it should be met and removed. And certainly we, in England, should not think we had far to go to find a grievance for the South in the Morrill tariff.[1] Speaking for myself, I must say that, were I a citizen of the South, I would resort to any measures, short of physical force, to rid myself of such an injustice as that tariff. Now here is a ground for concession. Why should not a party be formed in the *West* to offer to the South a guarantee in the event of a reunion against any more of these tariff oppressions. Let it be a fundamental law of the Union that, in future, no Customs duty shall exceed 10 per cent (excepting such cases as spirits, tobacco &c., where an excise tax is imposed . . .). This would give you in the end, a larger revenue than any scale of protective duties would yield. It would give a greater impulse to the prosperity of the whole country. Pennsylvania & New England would gain in common with the rest of the Union from the increased power of consumption, which would secure them the best market in the World at their own doors for all that they could produce. The West would have a constantly increasing market in Europe. The exports of provisions and breadstuffs would in a few years equal in value the exports of cotton. In fact such would be the prosperity, that these terms of peace would, in a pecuniary sense (not including the loss of life and limb) abundantly compensate for the sacrifices of the war.

Besides, such terms would inspire so much confidence in Europe, that the credit of your Government securities would derive a great improvement. In fact I know nothing else that will inspire any confidence in the minds of Capitalists in Europe; for people are quite alarmed at the unsound *protective* system which has gained ascendancy in your legislation and which we, in the old world, know, by long experience can only lead to impoverishment in the people and embarrassment in your finances. It is a discouraging fact for the advocates of popular self government throughout the world to see your Congress half a century behind our aristocratic House of Commons in all that relates to fiscal or politico-economical legislation.

Now is there any practical value in this suggestion? Is the South absolutely determined to refuse all offers for reconstructing the Union? Is the North bent on nothing short of the unconditional subjection of the South? If such be the spirit on both sides, there is no advantage whatever to be hoped for from any appeals to reason or sentiment or moderation. The only hope is in the early exhaustion of one or both parties. For the longer this dreadful & bloody struggle goes on, the more fearful will be the penalty paid by both parties . . .

I pray Heaven that you may be able to sheathe the sword . . .'

Cobden Papers 22, ff. 81–84.

iii   Letter from Richard Cobden, Midhurst, to John Cassell, 11 January 1863.

'. . . I look with horror on the butchery that is going on in America. I would have preferred to see the black man emancipated in any other

---

[1] The Morrill Tariff Act of 1861 inaugurated the United States policy of high protective duties.

way than by the sword. There is no good work which may not, I believe, be done by peaceful means, better than by war. But the South fired the first shot & the blood must be laid at its door. At all events I hope as the result of so many horrors we shall at least gain the redeeming measure of slave emancipation. And this seems more & more probable. The much despised "nigger" will I expect be at last the arbitrator in this great struggle. The whites will exhaust themselves & the black man will then step in and reap the fruits. Heaven grant it may be so. For although I should not have been disposed to drink Doctor Johnson's toast "Success to the next rising of the slaves", I am quite disposed to drink to their success now that their masters are the insurgents . . .'

Cobden Papers 54, ff. 29–30. The original letter is in
the British Museum, Add. MS. 43,671, ff. 48–51.

iv Letter from Richard Cobden, Midhurst, to James Caird, M.P., Langley Park, Beckenham, Kent, 3 November 1863.

'. . . I do not doubt what must be the result of the war, *the ruin & subjection of the Slave power.* If it were a contest between the North & a homogenous community of free men with a just grievance occupying the Southern States and contending for independence, I should look on the attempt to conquer them as the most chimerical dream that ever entered the human mind. But a confederation of Slave owners is an impossible enterprise in this year of our Lord. How can the South contend against the disadvantage of having the entire working population either neutral or hostile? Let us suppose that Sussex were at war with Hampshire & that the latter county had eliminated from its arm-bearing population all the labourers employed in tilling the land, in performing all the muscular toil of boatmen, carmen, porters, domestic servants, blacksmiths, carpenters &c. &c., that all these were not only to be reckoned as unavailable for the ranks of the army, but ready to rise against the other class if an opportunity offered. How do you suppose Hampshire with its upper classes alone could contend permanently against Sussex with its whole population to recruit from? Now that is the predicament of the South . . .'

Cobden Papers 54, ff. 22–23.

v Letter from Richard Cobden, Midhurst, to W. H. Osborn, [New York], 12 August 1864.

'. . . I would not have voted for initiating a war for the abolition of slavery, for I believe in the power of God to solve problems affecting the interests of humanity without calling the Devil to his aid in the form of a cruel and destructive war. But as the slaveholder has challenged you to mortal combat, and as you have enlisted the sympathies of the true friends of freedom everywhere as the opponents of slavery, I think with horror of the possibility of the civil war ending with a compromise on that question.

We should hide our heads or only walk through the back streets for the rest of our lives if you were to make peace on such terms. Better far be beaten in the field, than having conquered your enemy in a white skin, hand over the negro again to him as a chattel slave. *You* are not now responsible for the existence of slavery, but after the war, assuming you to be successful, the North will have the entire responsibility for the position of the black man. With these feelings I am delighted to hear of the progress you are making in anti-slavery sentiments.

69

But as a matter of mere selfish calculation you ought to put an end to slavery on your whole continent. There will be no peace so long as it endures. If you cannot live together with the slave-owner, you will not be able to live as next neighbours. I was struck with a passage in that very sagacious, almost prophetic work of De Tocqueville, "Democracy in America" where he speaks of the probable dangers to the union, & he alludes to the difference of *manners* to be created by slavery as one of the dangers. *Not the difference of interest, but the difference of manners.* Now this is the whole case. It is impossible for slave-owners to live on terms of political equality with a society of freemen. It is not their fault but their misfortune that they have been brought up in a manner which disqualifies them for the duties of such a life. If we had in London slavery on the south bank of the Thames & freedom on the north, & representatives of both sides met in our Guildhall, the slave-owners would bully and beat our Charles Sumners[1] just as they have done in Washington . . .'

Cobden Papers 22, no. 109.

vi Letter from Arthur Pickering, Boston, to Richard Cobden, 23 December 1861.

'. . . Born in Massachusetts, and a Boston Merchant, I offer you no apology for expressing to you my admiration of the able views that you have taken of our American troubles. In the year 1845, the writer was in England and was truly astonished at the amount of *ignorance* which he then found prevailing as to the United States.[2] I speak not only of commercial men, but of educated university men, of lawyers & divines, and it would seem as if there must have been some grave error in a system of Education which gives to intelligent Englishmen so little practical knowledge of a Country with which you have such colossal and intimate relations, both business pecuniary & political. Knowing these things, I should despair of getting a fair hearing before the British public, if I did not know that beneath all ignorance and prejudice there runs always a strong vein, for what every Englishman worthy of the name calls *fair play*. Now I ask you to form a moral Ring for the North & the South.

In the first place, words are sometimes things, and it was not without a meaning that the South coined the word *Secession* to "Hide the deep damnation of their taking off". The real word, and impartial history will so record it, is *Rebellion*. Now is there anything in the past history of the North, to justify a *Southern Rebellion*? any injustice, any tyranny, any disposition to crowd, any disposition even to take advantage of her Southern institutions? To all these questions we answer a thousand times, no. It is a notorious fact, that with less voters, less products, less amount of per capita taxes and larger pro-rata disbursements *in her region*, the South always has managed, until the late election of Mr. Lincoln, to have the political ascendancy. She, the South (by combination with a portion of the democracy of the North, familiarly called

---

[1] Charles Sumner, a United States senator, and Chairman of the Senate Foreign Relations Committee. He was one of the leading anti-slavery figures in the North.

[2] On the same issue Cobden wrote to Thomas B. Potter: 'Seeing how densely ignorant & prejudiced the ruling class of this country are upon everything relating to the United States . . .'. Letter, 10 December 1863, Cobden Papers 38.

dough-faces, because they truckled to the South),[1] shaped the laws to suit her own policy, filled the majority of all the civil, naval, & military offices with Southern men, men to whom I do no injustice, when I say, that they were neither so capable, nor so honest as *Northern men*. Remember too, that before the United States Courts of Law, open theoretically to the citizens of *all the States*, there was not the slightest chance of *justice* for a Northern man, or even a *hearing* in a *Southern District United States Court*. A band of those very gentlemanly & accomplished men (about whom the correspondent of the London Times, Dr. Russell, was so enthusiastic when he visited the South) with Revolvers in their pockets, and Bowie Knives sheathed in their Coat-Collars ready for sudden use,[2] would very politely intimate to the Northern lawyer, who had come to plead in open court a case, that it would be for his health & well being, to quit the State. And when, for the sake of peace, we submitted to these things, we were called "mean cowardly Yankees, whom you could not *kick* into a fight". Remember too that unpopular as he might be, *any Southerner* could appear & plead unmolested in our *Northern Circuit Courts*.

I assent without fear of contradiction that there never has been a time when *Southerners* were deprived of any right, either *before Congress* or *before the Courts, and they have the same rights today*. It is not difficult for an intelligent man to understand the primal law of our Government. All Englishmen are bred up with an intuitive respect for what is called the Constitution of England, but what that Constitution truly is, it would puzzle many of you to tell. But an American knows that "*We the People*" formed our fabric of Government and that the same primary principle runs through it all, the right of the *majority* to rule, according to the forms of law; and *equality to all* before the Law. You see it in the Government of every little Town in New England where open town meetings, presided over by three or four *Select Men*, as they are called, pass by vote the necessary laws. You find it a little more complex when you come to a large City . . . or when you come to a State . . . or finally to the representative wisdom of the United States in Congress assembled, all of whom are *elected* by a popular vote, in some particular district, as well as the *President of the United States*, who according to *forms of Law* is voted for, by *We the People*. Coming back to the point from which I started. Now *nowhere* in all this complex yet simple form of Government, is there *any provision* by which a minority, *however large*, can of *itself accede* or refuse to submit to the majority, which in other words, *is the Law*. If it were not so "Chaos might come again" & any village, town & hamlet might *decide*, and like the South ask "*to be let alone*". Before them, the tribunal of Justice, before the law & the world, the Southerners, stand convicted of *Treason & Rebellion*.

The Cabinet of England might have easily satisfied themselves of this fact, and also of a much graver one, that is, that all good & regular Governments everywhere the world over, *were interested* in sustaining our *Regular United States Government*, because it is not in the long run

---

[1] The dough-faces were Northerners who supported Southern policies over territorial expansion and slavery.

[2] James Henry Hammond of South Carolina made this phrase popular when he reflected the hysteria of December 1859 when Congress met just after the John Brown fiasco. Every Congressman came 'armed with a revolver—some with two—and a bowie knife'. Quoted by Nye & Morpurgo, vol. 2, *op. cit.*, p. 454.

the *interest* of European Governments to support the Southern doctrine of *Secession* or *Rebellion,* and still less is it their interest to acknowledge, *even as belligerants,* those who have not yet vindicated their title to anything but the names of *wicked traitors* & the Authors of an unnatural *Rebellion.*

You once had a Statesman who understood the value of securing the Friendship of the United States. I allude to Canning.[1] His famous sentiment "England & the United States, *Mother & Daughter against the World*" ought always to have been the *Keynote* of British statesmanship. However our present disputes may terminate, it requires no prophet to foretell that in the various complications of European politics, the time will come when you will repent in sack cloth & ashes, that in this domestic quarrel of ours, with which you had nothing to do, you have trampled upon our feelings, hurt our pride, wounded our *nationality* & given indirect aid & comfort to our Rebel enemies. A short time ago we received the Heir to your Throne with open arms.[2] Were he here today there would be "none so poor as do him homage". It is no slight thing to excite the *just enmity* of Twenty Two Millions of People such as we are, and as you have yourself remarked, with such a *tendency to growth.* You are right when you predicted that if you assumed the side of the South we should make a howling wilderness of it, rather than you should enjoy it . . .

Excuse me, but I am astonished at the double distilled stupidity of your Government. Rightly understood, our quarrel was a God-send to you. You had only to keep aloof, the longer it lasted the *better for you,* instead of foolishly throwing away money for *steamers, troops & munitions of war.* A liberal loan, say *Fifty Millions Sterling* devoted to *India*[3] for the *Cultivation of Cotton* & what you need quite as much, the *Encouragement of settlements of Colonists in India,* should have been your policy. A few years, and a liberal expenditure would make India a large *Consumer* as well as *Producer,* and build up also something to defend India with, against other than Indian Rebels. *Russia* has not forgotten the *Crimea* & the road to her revenge is through Persia, to your Indian possessions. There is another question of morals I should like to propose to you. As Individuals, States, Rail Road Companies &c. we owe your people a very large sum of money. Should your Government join the South, against us, the Southern Flag being to us a *Rebel* and *a Pirate Flag,* are we bound in *equity,* or *justice* ever to pay your principal or interest? . . . If you join the South, you become as bad as they, and in fact *do what they do.* Don't let the glorious old Flag of England be disgraced by such an alliance. Save your reputation, save your money (so much needed by your poor at home), save human life, so easy to take, so impossible to be restored. Save us, in the United States from devoting all our energies to the invention of machines to destroy rather than to benefit mankind.

---

[1] George Canning (1770–1827), former statesman and Foreign Secretary.

[2] The Prince of Wales (later King Edward VII) visited the United States in 1860. There are papers relating to this visit in the Lyons Papers in the West Sussex Record Office.

[3] Whilst some were advocating developing India as an alternative to the Southern states for cotton, others advocated developing the cotton trade with Central America. For the latter view see the printed letter of 25 January 1861 by E. G. Squier entitled *Is Cotton "King?": Sources of Cotton Supply* in the Lyons Papers.

A wise nation could easily find a substitute, for a time at least, for *Cotton*. Compound fabrics of Cotton & Wool, wool & silk and Cotton & Linen, also an increased supply of Linen Fabrics might be made to fill the vacuum, but it seems to me, who am only a merchant, that no one but a mad man would think of fighting 22 millions of People because Lancashire, or all England, fancies she needs Cotton. "The game is not worth a candle" more particularly when you do not know how long the candle may burn, *what it may light up*, and to crown all, when you do not know in the *end whose fingers may be most burned . . .*'

Cobden Papers 6, nos. 166–168.

vii Letter from J. B. Smith, London, to Richard Cobden, 17 January 1862.

'. . . For the Federals to give up the blockade of the South would be to give up the war. The blockade is the only means of distressing the South & shortening the contest. Give them arms, ammunition & such supplies as they could get in exchange for their cotton & you place them in a position that will enable them to bid defiance to the North. This I am persuaded the Federals will never do. If they can take possession of New Orleans & Mobile & by that means let out the cotton, but keep out arms, all well and good. I have a very strong opinion that it is our interest not to interfere in any way in the contest but let the contending parties fight it out. Any other course is certain to involve us in war.

If we acknowledge the South, "the chief corner stone" of whose govt. is professedly human slavery, whose leading men have advocated the conquest of Mexico & its conversion into a slave state & also the opening of the slave trade. Should we not with our constant boast that we have pd. 20 mills. for the abolition of slavery, & have spent as much more to put down the slave trade,[1] be justly branded with everlasting infamy as the rankest hypocrites?

But our acknowledgt. of the Confederates would not put an end to the Federal rights of blockade. To free the blockade would assuredly result in war. What quantity of cotton should we get in a state of war & at what price? What extremeties would not a war drive the Federalists to? Would they not raise the black population against us & rather burn all the cotton they can lay their hands on than that we should get it?

I look upon this struggle in Ama. as big with the most important consequences. We have had nothing like it since the French revolution & it may become equally bloody. The Federalists did not begin the war with the intention of abolishing slavery, but you know I have from the first thought that it might so eventuate. They would have acted wisely to have followed our example to have offered the Confederates 200 or £300 millions to abolish slavery, probably a less sum than the war will cost them. But the time for compromise is now past. The Federals have been unable to snuff out the rebellion in 6 months as they thought. The bitterest hatred exists between the combatants, & it is evident the war is fast *drifting* into an Anti-Slavery contest.

---

[1] In passing a measure for the abolition of slavery throughout the British colonies in 1833, Parliament had voted £20,000,000 compensation to the slave-owners.

Since the Federals have been unable to coerce the Confederates, will they not, rather than give up the contest, call in the aid of the slaves? If on the other hand the chances should change & the Federals should triumph will they be satisfied with letting matters fall into their old state & run the risk of another rebellion? Will they not rather reason that as Slavery lays at the foundation of the rebellion it will be better to settle the question at once than to run the risk of having to do the work over again hereafter. It appears to me, therefore, that whether the Federalists succeed in the war or not something will be done to settle the question of slavery for ever.

Now what is the condition of our cotton manufacturers? They have laughed at the idea of danger to the supplies of slave labor cotton from America & are caught at a moment when 85 p.c. of their whole consumption is from Ama. Hitherto the American growth has been as progressive as the increase of our manufactures, but looking at the altered state of things, will any sane man say that this can continue? On the contrary there can be no doubt for years to come the production under the most favourable circumstances will be very much reduced. What then is the best course to be pursued? Why, to quietly yield to the necessities of the position in which our own folly has placed us & to push the growth of cotton in the only country which can furnish the supplies we need, viz. India, & to press the govt. to take those steps which will best promote this object . . .'

Cobden Papers 7, nos. 20–21.

viii   Letter from W. H. Aspinwall,[1] Rockwood, Tarrytown, New York, to Richard Cobden, 11 September 1863.

'. . . I am quite sure that you will have rejoiced at the progress we are making towards the ending of this wicked war. As a distinguished statesman of Kentucky has recently written to me "This civil war which far seeing patriots could not avert, is fast exhausting the weaker party in the contest" & I think his remark applies to the moral, as well as to the physical view of the question. But he being a large slave-holder would probably not fully agree to this. The feeling is gaining ground here that any peace without the immediate or early abolition of slavery would disgrace us in the eyes of the world, & entail on us the probability of a repetition in after years of the sad experience we are going thro' at present that national sins bring national punishment.

I mean that this feeling is gaining with the moderate & conservative classes who were willing that things should remain as they were before the rebellion, looking upon slavery as an evil entailed on us & for which this generation was not responsible . . .'

Cobden Papers 7, no. 85.

ix   Letter from W. H. Osborn, Illinois Central Rail Road Company, New York, to Richard Cobden, 6 September 1864.

'. . . As to our resources for prosecuting the war we have a greater abundance of the essential supplies of food than we have had before for five years. Whether paper currency is sound or unsound is of little

---

[1] William Henry Aspinwall was one of New York's leading merchants, and reputed to be one of the richest men in the city. He acted as one of Lincoln's secret emissaries to England to urge the British government to stop the building of ironclads under construction for the Confederacy at the Laird shipyards.

74

consequence in prosecuting the war, as we lack no elements of strength within our own borders and have thus far experienced within our own borders none of the desolations of civil war, while in three-fourths of the Southern States there exists a complete chaos. The women are left at home, in large cities they resort to prostitution. The churches are closed. The schools do not exist and the youth of this generation are growing up in complete ignorance. There is no famine but there are epidemics and sickness, and the mortality among the black population seems to be as great among the whites.

The downfall of slavery seems to be coupled with as striking horrors as the downfall of eastern nations foretold by the prophet in the books of the Old Testament. Thus far the only state that seems to be willing to resume its peaceful pursuits under the Union is Louisiana, but in that state unfortunately both Cotton and Sugar promise very badly this season owing to the army worm.

The desperate virulence of the Southern people is shown by their inhuman treatment of our prisoners. They are today starving and shooting some thirty thousand (30,000) of them cooped up in a pen, thirty acres in extent, in a small town in Georgia . . .'[1]

Cobden Papers 7, nos. 138–139.

x   Letter from F. M. Edge, 49 Hanover Street, Pimlico, London, to Richard Cobden, 7 November 1864.

'. . . We have nothing, we never had anything, analogous to it[2] in Europe; and the rule by which we measure effects here is inoperative across the Atlantic. The very laws of population increase in the Old World are revolutionised in the New; and as though Providence were not satisfied with giving that Continent all our seasons and products, Americans are blessed with the Indian summer and inexhaustible rivers of oil. But, to my mind, and I think you will agree with me, this war, horrible as it appears, is the very greatest blessing ever bestowed upon a people. I do not say this from religious views merely, but from an economical point of thought; and I feel convinced that effects must supervene from this contest which will astound European statesmen. Until the election of Mr. Lincoln, the South has ruled the Union in the interests of agriculture, keeping manufactures and commerce—which really make a country—so much as possible in abeyance. One of their cardinal principles was (I mean of the South) that the Federal Govt. should not interfere with internal improvements, and without roads and canals it was almost impossible to develop the teeming resources of the Republic. When I left the U.S. in 1858, the Gas Companies of N.Y. city, Philadelphia and Boston were importing coal from Liverpool at from \$10 to \$20 per ton; and yet I, the son of the oldest living gas manufacturer, have seen coal there 50 per cent better for gas purposes than our best cannel.[3] Now it is a cardinal principle of the present dominant party to aid the States in public works, and this means bringing millions of quarters of grain to a market that now are burnt in steamboats and locomotives "out West", for want of sufficient means of intercommunication.

---

[1] This refers to Andersonville Prison, the largest and most notorious of the Confederate military prisons.
[2] He has previously referred to 'the wonderful state of things in America'.
[3] Cannel is a bituminous coal used in gas-making.

Hitherto we have had a species of triangular duel in America. The dominant South has been fighting the manufacturing and commercial East, and the agricultural and trading West, playing them off one against the other. Now the whole country is going to be *West*, which means Free Trade at a very early date; for what the West wants is rapid and easy exchanges—only possible under unrestricted commerce. Instead of a triangular duel of sections, we shall have *out of this war* an autocracy of the whole people. Lincoln was nominated at the West, by the West, and voted for by all the West, on a Western question —the Territories. The fighting has mainly been done by the West, and the successful generals are Western. Many of the sailors are from the West, beginning with old Farragut[1] from Tennessee.

The war is no harm to the country as regards human life, for all humanity is breeding for them faster than war can kill off. And the debt is a flea-bite . . . Wipe out the stupidity of slavery—capital owning labour—and such a stream of immigration must set into the Republic as history never knew. Consequently we shall have a division of taxation amongst greater numbers, and a vast increase of productive power; a Nation . . . possessing the trinity in unity of agriculture, manufactures and commerce in a higher degree of perfection than the world has ever seen . . .'

Cobden Papers 7, no. 168.

xi   Letter from J. D. Bradford, West Roxbury, [Boston], Massachusetts to Richard Cobden, 13 March 1865.

'. . . In the time of Sir Francis Burdett,[2] America was looked upon as a model government, but that day has passed away, and you and others have lived to see her in her present unhappy position, her union gone, the North contending with the South, and a civil war in progress, such as was never seen before. It was a remark of Robespierre in one of his speeches in 1792, "that liberty had no more deadly enemy than war". How signally has the truth of this remark been proved by the civil war with which this country is now engaged! How painfully have we been called to witness the violation of the constitution, the work of Washington, Jefferson, and other distinguished heroes of the revolution, and what a debt we have accumulated, which will already compare in magnitude to that of Great Britain, and is destined to bear with a weight too heavy to be borne upon the generations yet unborn. It seems impossible to conceive how men who are not insane, could have brought the country into this state, but it might all have been expected after the firing the first gun at Fort Sumter. I am glad that you are of the opinion that the war will not last much longer . . .'[3]

Cobden Papers 8, no. 111.

---

[1] Under the command of Captain (later Admiral) David Farragut, the navy made a vital contribution to the Union's strategy during the Civil War.
[2] 1770–1844.
[3] Within a few weeks the war was over with the fall of Richmond, the Confederate capital, on 2 April and General Lee's surrender at Appomattox on 9 April.

Englishmen in America

Nineteenth century America attracted an enormous number of travel writers and journalists, political and economic commentators, business men, speculators and adventurers. With its seemingly endless resources and almost limitless capacity for innovation, the American way of life was subject to the most intense scrutiny by visiting foreigners, anxious to understand for themselves what the American experiment was all about, how it worked and how it was getting on. They came to 'observe, describe, analyze and judge. No other people, it is safe to say, was ever so besieged by interpreters; none had its portrait painted, its habits described, its character analyzed, its soul probed so incessantly.'[1]

Many of the most important foreign writers on the American scene were from Britain: Mrs. Trollope (*Domestic Manners of the Americans*, 1832); Harriet Martineau (*Society in America*, 1836, and *A Retrospect of Western Travel*, 1838); Charles Dickens (*American Notes*, 1842); Alexander Mackay (*Western World*, 1849); Thomas Colley Grattan (*Civilised America*, 1859); Edward Dicey (*Six Months in the Federal States*, 1863); Matthew Arnold (*Civilisation in the United States, First and Last Impressions of America*, 1888); James Bryce (*The American Commonwealth*, 1888); George Warrington Steevens (*The Land of the Dollar*, 1898).

Two other visitors to America[2] were Richard Cobden, the politician, from Heyshott, near Midhurst in Sussex, and Frederick Ivor Maxse, a young army officer fresh from Sandhurst, whose family came to settle at Fittleworth in Sussex. Widely differing in personality, their approaches were from two totally different points of view. Cobden went to see as much of American life as he could—social, economic and political—and to do what he could to cement Anglo-American friendship on the political level. Young Maxse went for fun, for a holiday to Georgia, to enjoy a spot of hunting and adventure.

Richard Cobden[3] first toured the United States for just over a month in 1835, visiting the chief cities and towns of the East coast. In 1859 he returned, to spend a little over three months on a much more intensive and exhausting tour which took him much further westwards, this time to Chicago and the Mississippi to see the new prairie lands of the middle West. One of his main reasons for this tour was so that he could see for himself the line and management of the Illinois Rail Road Company in which he was a major shareholder. Extracts from his American diaries for both tours are given here,[4] in each case followed by extracts from correspondence he wrote home to England.

---

[1] Henry Steele Commager, *America in Perspective: The United States through Foreign Eyes* (1947, 10th impn. 1964), p. xii.

[2] Note that during the preparation of this anthology a further diary of an Englishman's American tour was deposited in the West Sussex Record Office. This was kept by Rear-Admiral C. M. Buckle and records his journey of 1885 which took in the East Coast cities and Chicago, St. Paul, Minneapolis, St. Louis and Cincinnati.

[3] See also above, pp. 65–76.

[4] His two American diaries are in the British Museum (Add. MSS. 43,807, A and B, and 43,808, A and B). There is an edited typescript of both in the West Sussex Record Office (Cobden Papers 444) the transcription of which is unreliable. The passages selected below have all been checked and corrected against the originals, although in parts some punctuation has been amended for this anthology. Note that these diaries have also been published as a study by Elizabeth Hoon Cawley in *The American Diaries of Richard Cobden* (1952).

i   Extracts from Richard Cobden's American diary, 1835.

'June 7, 4 a.m.
Are up by sun rise—open rejoicing & shaking of hands on the Approach of land—small vessels in the distance towards shore—eager look out for the pilot-boat which approaches us—beautiful sailing craft schooner-rigged—puts our pilot on board of us at 7—not like our pilots—all eyes criticize this first American visitor— . . . pass the narrows & enter the inner bay . . . What beauty will this inner bay of New York present centuries hence when wealth & commerce shall have done their utmost to embellish this scene! . . .

June 8
Henry[1] drives me into the country—vast extent of plan of New York & the high price of land which is sold in building lots even seven miles from the Town— . . . go on to Manhattan-ville, a small village with a primitive-looking little church with wooden spire—return by way of Haarlem bridge. Prodigious number of vehicles of all kinds that were pouring out into the country with company of every degree & color as we returned to New York. In England such a scene—in the neighbourhood of even London could only be observed on the occasion of some races in the vicinity— . . .

June 9
Take a trip on Long Island . . . Cross the Brooklyn ferry— . . . party comprised amongst others Judge Boardman . . . Undignified in contrast with the big wigs of our bench in England— . . . go to Coney Island . . . thence to Bath-House, another resort for holiday parties—we had a difficulty in making the driver go this extra distance. Our Judge threatened to throw him off & drive us if he did not comply— . . . the fire-fly or lightning-bug—the cricket—frogs & other insects & animals make the woods more noisy at night than day—My American friends anxious to draw comparison between England or Europe & America in favor of latter— . . . conceded that *"cherries do grow in England as good as in America"* as if that were a bit of praise— . . .

June 10
. . . Philadelphia a tame & uninteresting Town from the water—but with more appearance of maturity & stability than New York . . . beauty of water works— . . . blacks in the [theatre] gallery keep on one side & whites on the other . . . This has been the hottest day I ever knew.

June 11
. . . Baltimore is the handsomest place I have yet seen—here are the finest monuments—the prettiest girls and the Cleanest City in the Union— . . .

Am struck with the white & clean appearance of the linen & white clothes of all classes & colors—No poor people or beggars—The Theatre . . . not equal to that of Philadelphia—saw a man in the front seat of the dress circle with one foot hanging over into the pit . . .

---

[1] Henry Cobden, Richard's brother.

June 12

. . . Leave by the Coach for Washington at 8—A poor soil all the way—Companion outside a Virginian—his remark that the people could not live on that soil we were passing through except by breeding & selling slaves to the southern planters. Anecdotes of slavery—of the white ladies with mulatto offspring— . . . a fortune left to a mulatto family which cannot be possessed by it owing to the mother having been a slave—the Maryland laws do not allow free slaves to remain if manumitted in that state— . . . Approach to Washington not very remarkable — . . . at dinner twice as many slaves as the free waiters . . . the brushing away the flies by black boys with bunches of feathers during dinner reminded me of the West Indies— . . .

June 13

. . . leave Washington at 11 o'clock for Frederick—passing through George Town am shown the workhouse & told that the white & colored inmates have separate tables for meals.

Companions a blacksmith going to the West for work who can earn 18 dollars a month & be *"found"*—hours of working from sun rise till sunset or in winter say from sun-up till eight in the evening—all kinds of journeymen work more hours pr. day in America than in England—A lady & her companion who wore gold spectacles, who talked about taste & enquired of me about Bulwer, Lady Blessington & the Duke of Devonshire, but chewed tobacco & spat incessantly . . .

Heard today of instances of girls marrying in Maryland at 12 & 13 years of age—Still told that the part through which we are going *"raises"* great quantities of negroes for sale & some families are mainly indebted to this traffic for support— . . . the road all the way from Washington to Frederick is execrable & the dexterity with which the drivers carry a coach & four horses over roads that for ruggedness & occasional steepness surpass our Derbyshire cross-roads would be enough to make our English *jehus* marvel could they behold it . . .

June 14

. . . Our road from Frederick through Hagers Town, Cumberland & Union by the famous national turnpike has presented one continued scene of almost boundless forests of pine, oak che[s]tnut, locust etc. with only an occasional relief of a little cleared spot—the settlers on the borders of this great thoroughfare are very numerous & they appear industrious & prosperous— . . . this is Sunday & the Sabbath day is as strictly kept in these woods as in England—saw some negroes going out on horseback well dressed.

My companion . . . tells me he has been to Baltimore with his black groom who is riding outside . . . his kindness to his man George who is a handsome & smart negro—the night is cold & George at the request of his master is squeezed inside with us—he is quite at his ease—George dines in the same room as ourselves but at a separate table— . . .

June 15

Passing over the last summit of the Alleghanies . . . looked down upon a plain country, the beginning of that vast extent of territory known as the great Mississippi valley & which extends almost without variation of surface to the base of the Rocky Mountains, & increasing in fertility

& beauty the further it extends westward—here will one day be the headquarters of agricultural & manufacturing industry. Here will one day center the civilization, the wealth, the power of the entire world— . . . We are now in the State of Pennsa. Thank God I am no longer in the country of slaves.

June 16

. . . the whole distance from Brownsville to Pittsburgh we see the mouths of coal pits opening upon the road on the edge of the water—great probable value of this district at some future period.

First place we stop at for Coals[1] farmed by two Englishmen who paid two thousand dollars for the use of the pit, which debt they discharged by the produce of coals last year & have cleared one thousand dollars besides— . . . one of them observed to me that he wished he had left England ten years earlier . . .

Graham, an Irish emigrant on board who came out 16 years ago without money as a journeyman carpenter & is now worth he says 16,000$—speaks unfavorably of his countrymen who come to America —his honest defence of the country of his birth against every one seeking to disparage her— . . . bustle of the Town of Pittsburgh as we approach — . . . number of splendid Ohio Steam boats lying at anchor— . . . ascend Grants Hill—view of the Town, probably one day destined to be the largest in America— . . . Our friend [Mr. Graham] . . . takes us to view a cotton factory belonging to Allen who he told us had come to this continent from Ireland after failing in business & had returned thither to satisfy his creditors—handsome brick structure . . . 4,500 spindles, & power looms for coarse sheetings—employ about 180 people—hours from five in the morning till half past six in the evening—the children from nine upwards earn from 6s/6d to 8s/6d weekly[2]. . . —Evening, sup with friend Graham . . . Go to the theatre— . . . enthusiasm with which republican sentiments were caught up—"No crowned head in Christendom can boast that he ever commanded for one hour the services of this arm" a phrase which was rapturously cheered . . .

June 17

. . . pass through the German village of Economy . . . the establishment was founded by Rapp—on the principle of Owen of Lanark[3]—go into the house—clean appearance of the interior—the inmates appeared to me to exhibit the dull sunken eyes & the *sodden* inflexible features peculiar to all fanatics— . . . observe not one black face throughout the day's journey—the Ohio law prohibits people of color from entering this state except under particular regulations—the children ever

---

[1] They were on board the steamboat *Fancy*.

[2] Or 32½p to 42½p.

[3] George Rapp had emigrated to America to escape religious persecution in Germany. With his followers he founded the Harmony Society and established a model community, New Harmony, in Indiana. In 1824 the village was sold to the Scottish industrialist and utopian socialist, Robert Owen, where he conducted his own social experiments. Rapp moved to Pennsylvania to set up a new model community at Economy, north of Pittsburgh. (Note that in 1843 Owen communicated his ideas for social reform to Cobden. As President of the Congress of the Rational Society he sent Cobden an address advising him to be less single-minded about economic reform. Instead there should be a deep-rooted reform of society. For this address, signed by Owen, see Cobden Papers 586.)

since we passed the Allegheny Mountains have struck us as remarkably
healthy & lovely—the population more robust than the inhabitants
of the maritime Towns— . . . Poland is a pretty thriving little Town
chiefly of wood with two or three good brick houses quite in the English
style—Ohio, free from the curse of slavery or of the presence of a
black population, is advancing with greater prosperity than any State
of the Union— . . .

June 18
Our party inside is now increased to nine persons—converse on the
Bank, slavery, and as usual on land investments & internal improvements—have remarked that politics are rarely discussed in public
conveyances—Here I found, as in every other company, the slavery
blot viewed as an indelible stain upon & a curse to the country—an
intelligent old gentleman would prefer the debt of Great Britain to
the colored population of the United States—all agree in the hopeless-
ness of any remedy as hitherto proposed . . . bad state of the roads—
obliged to walk part of the way— . . . pass through Monroe, Kinsman
& to Connéaut on Lake Erie where we arrive at 8 o'clock in the
evening, having been forty hours in travelling by mail 110 miles— . . .

June 19
Start at six . . . by the William Penn Steamer for Buffalo— . . . converse
with an old man who appears familiar with the business of settling a
new country—Hints for emigrants—a man & wife with family finding
themselves in Illinois or Indiana or Michigan [are] certain of comfort
& ultimate wealth provided they are industrious & possess a capital of
about a hundred pounds—say, buy a government lot of eighty acres
at 5s/. per acre[1] (a credit is given)—two good horses called a team may
be had for twenty pounds—or a yoke of oxen for ten pounds—sow a
few acres for present subsistence of maize, wheat & potatoes. These
& cow will yield a maintenance for the first year—Neighbours assist
to build the log hut of the new-comer—furniture may be had &
carried in an unfinished state from New York or Albany. Shopkeepers
in the nearest Town take produce for goods—if an emigrant is acquainted with a retail business as well as with farming & is active it
gives him a better chance— . . .

June 21
[At Buffalo] breakfast with a party of about eighty at seven—go to
walk afterwards in the Town which is a thriving place that has sprung
up since the last war, during which the British destroyed this place[2]—
handsome wooden church—the principal street superior to anything
in Pittsburgh—go at ½ past 8 by rail road to the ferry two miles &
thence cross to Canada in the first cattle-tread wheel boat I ever saw
. . . take a coach after reaching the Canada shore & proceed to the
falls of Niagara— . . . Church[3] remarks that even the *"martin houses"*
are in Canada inferior to those in the U. States— . . . reach the Pavilion
Hotel near the falls at one—go immediately to see this greatest of
natural wonders alone—I jealously guard my eyes from wandering
until I find myself on the Table Rock—thank God that has bestowed
on me health, time & means for reaching this spot . . .

[1] Or, 25p per acre.
[2] Buffalo was razed to the ground in December 1813.
[3] A fellow traveller, from Pittsburgh.

June 23

Rainbow nearly a complete circle seen from Table Rock—cross again to the American side . . . take a bath, not one on the Canada side— . . . were I an American I would here strive to build me a summer residence —in the evening drunken people—have seen more intoxicated persons at this first Canada Town than in any place in the States . . .

July 6

Leave Boston at 9 morng. for Lowell by the rail road— . . .

Go over a woollen mill for power loom weaving, a good establishment— all the looms are worked by girls . . . The hours here as in all the other factories are from five in the morning till seven at night with an hour & a half for meals—see the whole of the girls in the village go home to dinner—their orderly & superior manner as compared with our young women of the same class.

Go to see the machine shop . . . remark on the cleanliness of the men who are all neatly shaved,—Mr. Prince tells me that no man goes home to dinner without washing—*even the Irish* always wash before leaving his work shop . . .

In the eveng go to Mrs. Inglis to see her children perform "a play of the Corsair" . . .

Eaves-dropping a propensity in this country. Dr. Wilsone & I are earwigged by a fellow in fashionable disguise.

July 7

. . . Leave Boston at 4 p.m. for the rail road— . . . the carriage takes fire . . . Pat souses us with water from the roof—his glee at our trouble— "Oh! tis noting—tis notin[g]"—The Yankees are too much in a hurry to finish things properly before they "go ahead"— . . .

July 9

. . . The stores [in New York] handsomer than anything in England— built with granite fronts to the ground floor. Very open & light & the goods are exposed on the bottom floor—Pearl St. & Pine St. will at some future time be the two best streets of warehouses in the world unless Manr.[1] should very much improve the taste of her buildings . . .

July 14

. . . to Hoboken—*bars* everywhere—at the ferry resting-place—on board the ferry—in the gardens of Hoboken etc. etc. Wherever there is a concourse of Americans you will find a bar & in truth with such a hot climate the people are excusable in drinking. I have today per- spired pints & have swallowed quarts of water—the thermometer 96 in shade—Hoboken a retired country retreat used much for children to walk in during the morning & in the afternoon the resort of multi- tudes of Cocknies from New York—on a Sunday tens of thousands of visitors sometimes cross in the Hoboken ferry boats— . . . beauty of this scene—N. Yk. the pleasantest situation in the U. States & perhaps in the world in respect to the surrounding attractions & facilities for making excursions of health or pleasure . . .

---

[1] Manchester.

. . . to Staten Island . . . a beautiful view of the Bay of N. Yk. The Quarantine Station where the vessels from all parts are lying—the custom here is for the cabin passengers to proceed up to N. Yk. immediately on arrival by steam, and the steerage passengers if they exceed 40 in number are detained till their clothes are washed & the medical searcher pronounces them free from disease . . .'

Cobden returned, as he had arrived, in the sailing ship *Britannia*, leaving New York on 16 July. They landed at Liverpool on 16 August, Cobden closing the diary 'gratefully acknowledging the blessings of Providence in conducting us to terra firma. Amen.'

Cobden Papers 444, and British Museum Add. MS. 43,807, A and B.

ii Letter from Richard Cobden, Boston, to his brother Frederick in England, 5 July 1835.

'. . . My journey may be called a real *pleasure* trip, for without an exception or interruption of any kind I have enjoyed every minute of the *too too* short time allowed me for seeing this truly magnificent country. No one has done justice to the splendid scenery of America. Her lakes, rivers, forests, and above all her cataracts are peculiarly her own, and when I think of their superiority to all that we own in the old world and, still more, when I recollect that by a mysterious ordinance of their creator these were hid . . . till modern times I fell into the fanciful belief that the Western Continent was brought forth at a second birth and intended by nature as a more perfect specimen of her handy work. But how in the name of *breeding* must we account for the degeneracy of the human form in this otherwise mammoth producing soil? The men are but sorry descendants from the noble race that begot their ancestors; and as for the women! My eyes have not found one resting place that deserves to be called a wholesome, blooming, pretty woman since I have been here. One fourth part of the women look as if they had just recovered from a fit of the jaundice, another quarter would in England be termed in a state of decided consumption and the remainder are fitly likened to our fashionable women when haggard and jaded with the dissipation of a London season. There! haven't I *outtrolloped* Mrs. Trollope and *overhauled* even Basil Hall.[1]

But leaving the *physique* for the *morale*. My estimate of American character has improved, contrary to my expectations, by this visit, great as was my previous esteem for the qualities of this people. I find myself in love with their intelligence, their sincerity, and the decorous self-respect that actuates all classes. The very genius of activity seems to have found its fit abode in the souls of this restless and energetic race. They have not, 'tis true, the *force* of Englishmen in personal weight or strength, but they have compensated for this deficiency by quickening the momentum of their enterprises. All is in favour of celerity of action and the saving of time. Speed, speed, speed, is the motto that is stamped in the form of their ships and steam boats, in the breed of their horses and the light construction of their waggons and carts, and in the ten thousand contrivances that are met with here . . . All is in pursuit of one common object—the economy of time . . .

---

[1] Both had written scathingly about American manners and customs a few years before.

You know I predicted when leaving England for this continent that I should not find it sufficiently to my taste to relish a sojourn here for life. My feelings in this respect are quite altered. I know of no reasonable ground for an aversion to this country, and none but unreasonable minds could fail to be as happy here as in England provided friendly attachments did not draw them to the "old country" . . .

. . . They are the most insatiable gourmands of flattery and praise that ever existed. I mean praise of their country, its institutions, great men, etc. . . . I consider this failing—perhaps as a good phrenologist I might almost term it a disease—to be an unfortunate peculiarity. There is no cure for it, however. On the contrary it will go on increasing with the increase of the wealth, power and population of the United States, so long as they are *United*, but no longer. I have generally made it a rule to parry the enquiries and comparisons which the Americans are so apt to thrust at an Englishman. On one or two occasions when the party has been numerous and worth powder and shot, I have . . . found the only method of allaying their inordinate vanity . . . by resorting to this mode of argument: "I admit all that you or any other person can, could, may or might, advance in praise of the past career of the people of America. Nay more. I will myself assert that no nation ever did, and in my opinion none ever will, achieve such a title to respect, wonder and gratitude in so short a period . . . And now I must add . . . that fifty years are too short a period in the existence of nations to entitle them to the palm of history. It is the biography of an individual, not the history of a great people, that can be comprised in *that brief* interval of time. No wait, the ordeal of wars, distresses and prosperity . . . which centuries of duration are sure to bring to your country, these are the test. And if many ages hence your descendants shall be able only to say of their country as much as I am entitled to say of mine *now*, that for seven hundred years we have existed as a nation, constantly advancing in liberty, wealth and refinement, holding out the lights of philosophy and true religion to all the world, presenting mankind with the greatest of human institutions in the trial by jury, and that we are the only modern people that for so long a time withstood the attacks of enemies so heroically that a foreign foe never put foot in our capital except as a prisoner (this last is a poser). If many centuries hence your descendants will be entitled to say something equivalent to this, then, and not till then, will you be entitled to that crown of fame which the historian of centuries is entitled to award." . . . In a general way, however, I find that this species of self-glorification is going out of fashion even with the less educated.

There is only one *trollopism* that I cannot reconcile my prejudices to. It is the nasty propensity for spitting . . . I could forgive their habit of smoking *for your sake*, and even the chewing of tobacco amongst the rude backwoodsmen who can make the "whole plantation" a spittoon might be looked over, but to find oneself in the streets of the cities, in the bars, or news rooms, constantly surrounded by well-dressed young men who "tchit" from between their teeth this filthy juice to the risk of your "pants" and boots is unpardonable. I sat in the same news room with three snipe-faced spitters of the first chop the other day, and they had a trough placed at about three yards distance into which they kept an incessant fire . . . I enjoyed the diabolical satisfaction as I looked at these performers to think that they would be all dead before I again visited this country, for they had already very nearly expectorated their Yankee souls up.

One of the best sights here after Niagara falls is the State Prison at Auburn. I was interested to find in the centre of a people governing themselves by universal suffrage . . . a penitentiary where the discipline is more rigorous and more terribly irksome than any that can be met with under even the most absolute despotisms. When I was at Auburn it contained 640 prisoners, not one of whom was allowed to open his lips whilst within its walls to speak to his fellows, but at the certain price of instant chastisement. They were all busily employed in several large workrooms, and I never saw men work so well. But there was something so absolutely appalling to my feelings in seeing so many being struck mute, as it were, and deaf also, that I almost felt the same sympathy with them as though they had been deprived of their tongues and ears by the orders of a cruel tyrant. Nothing but the consciousness that the punishment I was witnessing had a reforming tendency reconciled me to its dreadful severity. The prison contains 25 women, but the keeper said the system had been abandoned with them. It had been found *impossible* to make them keep silence!!¹

I witnessed the celebration here yesterday of the 4th July. There was the usual firing and parading of muskets. The usual appearance of the young ladies when soldiers are to be seen, and then there was the usual oration in the church, all of which I took care to see and hear. But I could not see the usual drunkenness of great fete days in England, nor were my ears dinned with the swearing and bawling in the style of our most moral countrymen. The temperance societies have certainly wrought wonders here. They were not put under the shade of ridicule as they have been, I fear, in Britain. I find this town is a great deal more like the "Old Country" than any place I have been in on this side, and the people bear a corresponding resemblance in their manners, characters and habits to their ancestors . . .'

Cobden Papers 20, ff. 216–223.

iii   Extracts from Richard Cobden's American diary, February–June 1859.

Cobden left Liverpool by the Cunard company's steamer *Canada* for Boston, via Halifax, Nova Scotia. This time the crossing by steamer took exactly fourteen days compared with the month's voyage by sailing ship when he returned home from New York in the 1830s. This tour, far more exhausting than the last, took him from the cities of the East coast as far West as Chicago and down the Mississippi to Memphis.

'*March 17 and 18*

Left Chicago in the morning with Mr. Osborn and Capn. Mclellellan² for Cairo by the branch of the Illinois Central Railroad, having the Directors' car & sleeping at night in the car in a "siding", & being

---

¹ This brief description by Cobden should be compared with Charles Dickens' description of the Eastern Penitentiary in Pennsylvania, based on the principle of solitary confinement. See his *American Notes* (1842), chapter 7.

² W. H. Osborn was President of the Illinois Central Rail Road Company, and George B. McClellan Chief Engineer and a Vice-President. Before retiring from the army in 1857, McClellan had been a military engineer with a good Mexican War record. At the outbreak of the Civil War he rejoined the army and distinguished himself in the early campaigns.

85

brought forward the following day to Cairo.—After passing over 20 or 30 miles we came upon the Great Prairie over which the road was carried four years since when there was scarcely an inhabitant upon it.—Now it is dotted with small farm houses built of wood.—Not a tree is visible, excepting here & there a few fruit trees around the houses.—The soil is a very rich black mud almost impassable in wet weather, there being no stones or other materials for roads.—The men wear boots outside of their loose trowsers, and with their long hair & beards they remind me more of Poles or Wallachians than members of the Anglo-Saxon family . . .

We reached Cairo in the evening of the 18th.—This Embryo City which stands on the tongue of land at the junction of the Ohio & Mississippi & which from its situation may be expected to be some day a populous seat of commerce, was almost a sheet of water owing to the overflow of the rivers.—There was at one house a ladder standing which offered to the inhabitants the opportunity of escaping from the first floor in case of a sudden flood, & a boat was moving from one wooden hut to another, the only mode of communication.—Half of a brick hotel had been swept away during the late storm, & we were glad to sleep in our railway carriage.—Still, notwithstanding the disasters from flood & fire which Cairo has gone through, to say nothing of its threatened dangers from earthquake, & despite of the ridicule which tourists & novelists have heaped on it,[1] I predict that its favorable site will lead eventually to the creation of a great commercial mart at Cairo. In walking through the accessible parts of the town & taking some supper at the wooden building called a hotel, I observed that the people had a wild amphibious aspect, wearing high boots outside of their trowsers & which seemed never to have been cleaned, whilst their long hair & beards gave them a Sclavonic aspect.—

March 19

Left Cairo in the morning by a large Mississippi Steamer for Memphis . . .

Stopped at Hickman, a town in Kentucky, from whence tobacco is largely shipped.—Went on shore to see the process of packing the tobacco in hogsheads, & found myself for the first time among a gang of slaves. A number of small negro boys were employed in carrying the tobacco from one room to another, & as we entered the premises we found the white overseer engaged in the characteristic employment of whipping one of these urchins.—This little river port, from which I was told a large amount of produce, the growth of a very rich tract of country, is shipped for New Orleans, presented a most neglected appearance.—It reminded me in many respects of a Spanish Town. Four mules were required to draw a cask of tobacco through the deep mud of the streets, which might be made perfectly hard for a few

---

[1] Dickens, in his *American Notes* (1842), also describes his trip down the Mississippi (see chapter 12). Of Cairo he wrote: '. . . we arrived at a spot so much more desolate than any we had yet beheld . . . At the junction of the two rivers, on ground so flat and low and marshy, that at certain seasons of the year it is inundated to the house-tops, lies a breeding-place of fever, ague, and death . . . A dismal swamp, on which the half-built houses rot away . . . the hateful Mississippi circling and eddying before it, and turning off upon its southern course a slimy monster hideous to behold . . . a place without one single quality . . . to commend it: such is this dismal Cairo'.

hundred pounds.—The people had a sort of slouching Spanish air,—
& even their hats & their high-pommelled saddles had a similar
resemblance.—

Senator Jefferson Davis from Mississippi was on board.[1]—A very
intelligent man though a strong advocate of Slavery and Southern
rights.— He had been Secretary at War in Taylor's administration, &
bore the reputation of being a very able & honest administrator . . .
Since I arrived in the States I have dined at large table d'hotes in all
parts, & have never seen a drop of anything but water drunk with the
dinner.—Here on board the Steamer we have no other beverage than
the muddy water of the river.[2] . . . Observed that the ladies on board
occupied one extremity of the large saloon which extended from almost
end to end of the vessel, & none of the male portion of the Community—
excepting those who accompanied the ladies on board, seemed any
more to presume to join them than if they had been in their own drawing
room.—The real deferential respect paid to women & the solid privileges accorded to them is apparantly as much the characteristic of this
country now as it was when I was here in 1835.—

March 20
. . . Holly Spring is a neat little town with 2,500 inhabitants, & containing many pretty white wooden houses.—After dinner, as I sat along
with a group of Citizens at the door of the inn, an old man of the party
informed me that he "let" his negro men for 240 dollars a year, the
hirers finding them in clothes and victuals.—I was also told by a
railway engineer that he paid for the hire of slaves (of course to their
masters) 20 dollars a month, finding them in food, but not in clothing.—
To skilled negro mechanics he paid from 4 to 500 dollars a year.—The
food he gave to these hired negroes is as follows—5 lbs of bacon a week,
a peck of Indian meal . . . a quart of treacle, a lb of tobacco . . . 1 lb
soap, salt . . .

March 25
Dunleith, the terminus of the Illinois Central railway on the Upper
Mississippi, stands on a high bank of the river opposite to Dubuque.—
Crossed over to the latter . . . In walking up to the heights at the back
of the town met a person carrying a bag of shavings, whom we accosted
by accident, & he turned out to be a well-educated intelligent person
who took us to his genteelly-furnished house, & afterwards accompanied
us to see the schools of the town.—In the "ward" school for primary
instruction there were eleven rooms in which boys and girls were
taught together.—With one exception the teachers were all females
who seemed to perform their duties in a very efficient manner.—Was
told their salaries were from 35 dollars to 50 dollars a month.—The
children were of all classes, blacksmiths' sons and physicians' daughters
performing the same tasks together.—On inquiry was told that the
practice of teaching the children of both sexes together was more &
more in favor.—In regard to the mixture of classes Mr. Spalding
observed that public opinion in America would frown down any
attempt at exclusiveness, that there had been an attempt to create a

[1] Davis was to become the President of the Confederate States of America during the
Civil War.
[2] Compare Dickens in his *American Notes*. He reported that when on the Mississippi in the
1840s (chapter 12): 'We drank the muddy water of this river . . .'

"codfish aristocracy" but it had quite failed.—"Every boy in this school", said he, "is eligible to become the President of the United States".—

Then went to the High School, where youths were completing the higher branches of study.—Found on the ground floor a very lady-like superior person who had young people of both sexes under her. Youths with moustaches & full grown young women were in the room.—Her moral influence & very superior attainments seemed to surmount the apparent disadvantages of her sex.—She told me she preferred teaching boys to girls as they were more ready & comprehensive in imbibing instruction. In an upper room we found also boys and girls being taught together . . . Was told that there are scarcely any private schools in Dubuque—that all classes attend these schools.—Heard the boys declaim from Grattan, Patrick Henry, etc. . . .

Went on board the Steamer the "War Eagle" & left for St. Louis . . . A number of emigrants for the new gold diggings at Pikes Peak came on board with their waggons and oxen, commencing a journey of upwards of 1,200 miles.[1] . . .

March 26 and 27

. . . The company on board the Boat comprised a great many rough bearded men with coarse dresses of uncouth fashion, some with loose trowsers tucked into their dirty boots, others with their pantaloons rolled up above their shoes like our "navigators".—These men, most of them young & full of animal spirits, were on their way to the new gold mines at Pikes Peak, all of them carrying the baggage & provisions & small fire arms required for a journey across the plains to the foot of the Rocky Mountains. I was struck with the orderly, sober & forbearing demeanor of these men.—Not a rude or boisterous word fell from any of them.—This I attribute to the sobriety of all on board.—With only one exception I observed that nothing but water was drunk at the table.—Everybody smoked & chewed tobacco, but these habits, however nauseous to others, are sedative in their influence on the temper of those who indulge in them.—It is the drinking of intoxicating liquors which leads to excitement and collisions.—Such a company as I find on board this boat, if assembled together in England under similar circumstances, with the incessant drinking of beer & spirits which would be resorted to for companionship & pastime, would be attended with boisterous rudeness, & inevitable collisions. The superior education in America will be thought by some, and the concealed bowie knife & revolver will be said by others, to account for the courtesy & forbearance of my fellow passengers, but I think the absence of stimulants to be the one great preserver of the peace.—

March 28

. . . As we went on shore at St. Louis we found a row of stately steamers at the quay extending almost a mile in length, & the wharves were encumbered with all kinds of produce & merchandise ready to be put on board.—Many of these vessels had notices hung out that they were destined for the Missouri and Pikes Peak, the newly-discovered El Dorado to which so many adventurous spirits were now pressing

---

[1] A reference to Pikes' Peak gold rush of the late 50s when thousands of prospectors were swarming to Colorado.

forward, probably in most cases to be grievously disappointed.—We were told that the emigration for these gold regions was probably as great as 2,000 persons a day, but this is probably an exaggeration.

The city of St. Louis is, in the solidity of its buildings, the extent of its commerce, & the reputed wealth of its capitalists, the third in importance in the States.—I have seen no place in the interior which gives the same impression of solid wealth & extensive commerce.—It is the centre from which nearly all the trade & emigration for the Great West radiates . . .

Here, as in nearly all the towns on the Mississippi, I observed that the most prominent & conspicuous looking buildings are the colleges & schools . . .

March 29

Arrived at Chicago at noon . . .

March 30

Was driven . . . through the city & along Michigan Avenue, the principal street leading into the country with good residences, some of them of stone, stretching for more than two miles to the south of the city . . . This city is said to contain more than 100,000 inhabitants, & is literally the growth of 30 years—surpassing in the rapidity of its increase any place in America, with the exception of St. Francisco.— The principal streets contain some shops & warehouses rivalling in style, and far surpassing in rental, anything to be found in London or Liverpool . . .

March 31

. . . On returning in a carriage . . . to the house of Mr. Arnold, & observing a collision in the muddy streets between two waggons, & remarking on the very great forbearance & courtesy of the drivers towards each other, the question arose as to what was the cause of this respectful demeanor under the most trying circumstances of the American working population.—My companion, the banker, started the theory that the fact of every man hoping & expecting to rise, gave to them the manners of those of a superior grade in society.—An ingenious & perhaps to some extent a correct theory.

In the evening was entertained at a dinner by the principal people in the city . . . Everybody in America seems endowed with the faculty of speaking in public with self-possession . . .

April 2

. . . Saw the process of raising a large brick hotel of about 100 feet frontage.— 800 screws are put under the building, & a man gives a turn to one after another.—This is going on with a larger number of workmen at the bottom of the building, whilst the inmates above are following undisturbed their usual avocations.—

April 19

. . . New York.—Passed through the Central Park which was being laid out & the roads formed.—About 700 or 800 acres have been purchased at a forced valuation in the centre of the island, & which will cost 5 to 7 million dollars, whilst the laying out & planting are expected to come to as much more. There is to be a lake of 120 acres to serve as a reservoir for the Croton water to supply the city.—The

money for this outlay is to be provided by taxation on the Town.—The
ground intended for the park is uneven & rocky, & admits of being
laid out with much beauty & will form, when planted and completed,
one of the largest & most beautiful parks in the world . . .'

From New York, Cobden went back to Chicago via Philadelphia,
Washington, Cincinnati, Indianapolis and Centralia. He then returned
to New York again, via Buffalo, and then headed north through Boston
to Canada where he visited Montreal and Quebec. He left Quebec for
England on 18 June in the screw-propellor *Indian*, sighting Ireland on
28 June. 'Our last view of the coast of Labrador was on the 21st . . .
consequently we have taken seven days to make the passage between
the two continents.'

*Cobden Papers 444, and
British Museum Add. MS. 43,808, A and B.*

iv   Letter from Richard Cobden, 'On the Mississippi between Cairo &
Memphis', to James Caird, M.P., Langley Park, Beckenham, Kent,
20 March 1859.[1]

'. . . I came from Chicago south to get into fine weather . . . I must now
tell you the impression the trip over 365 miles of Illinois made on me.

In the first place I was struck with the number of houses already put
upon the great Prairie. In many places there seemed to be as many
farm houses, though of a very different character, as in Norfolk or
Lincoln when away from the towns. But with all that I confess that as
an abode these treeless waste-looking plains would not be to my taste.
I could only get reconciled to them as a place for money making by the
manufacture of corn & meat for which ends they offer more tempting
investments than perhaps any spots on the globe. But when I came to
the half-wood and half-prairie country between Mattoon & Centralia
I confess I was quite taken aback by the tempting & beautiful scene.
I passed over nearly 100 miles of this land where open tracts of various
sizes . . . were bounded by belts of forest or interspersed with clumps of
trees, the most beautiful wheat land just laid out for the plough,
without a stump, stone or tree. Just, in fact, in the state in which good
farmers in England are anxious to have their farms & for which they
offer £2 a year rent. I confess when I saw this tempting scene I ex-
claimed "If I were a young man with a few hundred pounds at my
disposal & had my way to make in life, here I would pitch my tent for
the rest of my days".

The scenery in this part of Illinois is so completely English, so like what
I have seen in Yorkshire & Nottinghamshire, that it would not seem
like exile from my native land to live there . . .'

Cobden Papers 54, ff. 9–12.

v   Extracts from Frederick Ivor Maxse's American holiday diary, July–
September 1882.

Having just completed his officer training at the Royal Military College,
Sandhurst, Maxse left England with three friends, Crutwell, Giles and
'Cracker' Wise, bound for St. Simons Island on the coast of Georgia.

---

[1] Cobden also wrote the greater part of another letter to [?William] Sale whilst on the
Mississippi, dated 26 March 1859, in which he gives his impressions of the prairies
and the effect of the building of the railway. British Museum, Add. MS. 43,669, ff.
198–199.

Leaving Liverpool by the *Wyoming* on 29 July they docked at New York on 8 August where they seem to have been immediately duped by their coachman:

'*8 August*
. . . We are heckled on landing by one of those sharp-witted New Yorkers against whom we have been warned. He calls himself a baggage commissioner . . . This man puts us into a capital cab, for the St. Nicholas Hotel . . . We get into the cab: we are surprised to see the coachman get off his box, and ask to be paid beforehand—$1. I protest, but Giles gives the man an English sovereign. He gets two silver pieces in return. The man jumps up to the box and we rattle through the town. The change that the man has given Giles is worth about 1 shilling . . . I consol him by laughing at him & saying "I told you so". Giles says "Oh, I can get the rest back from the cabman when we get there". Of course the cabman laughs at Giles and pretends that the fare is 1 dollar each as he drives off with a grin . . .

The St. Nicholas Hotel surprises us with its splendour—& all for $3\frac{1}{2}$ dollars a day including 4 huge meals . . . Being too late for dinner we have to wait for "supper" at 9 p.m. What a remarkable meal it is, with . . . 10 or 12 dishes of wh. you may eat as many as you like! . . . After this portentous meal we adjourn to billiards, cigars & iced drinks. After this to bed.

The heat is indeed overpowering, but not so hot as I had expected. I sleep (outside my bed) well through the night. I am half afraid to get inside the bed, after my experience of the last 10 days, during wh. time my tender flesh has been a prey to the most dreadful bed insects of the larger kind.

9 August
. . . I go to Maitland and Phelps the bankers. All I know is that it is in a street 2 miles down Broadway, and that I can't afford to be cheated by a cabman. There is nothing like personal experience, and so in happy ignorance I get into the 1st "Stage" or buss that I meet going in the required direction. The Stage is quite full but I am not bashful & so I sit on the step. There is no conductor to the stage, only a coach-man. I hear a voice behind me telling me to get in a bit. I get up and stand inside between peoples' legs, and catch hold of a bar on the roof. I learn all this by looking in the looking glass . . . I ask a man near me if I am right for Exchange Place. He says it is the wrong bus for that. I then ask how I am to pay. My friend points to a box and asks me if I have got any money. He then points to another bus and tells me to run and get in there. He says never mind paying. I do so. I get into this stage as if I had been accustomed to it all my life: it is full but I get in, shove between peoples' legs and hold on to the roof. I see a man touch a nob & ring a bell, at wh. the coachman puts his hand through a hole, receives a piece of silver from the passenger and gives the latter a paper in return. I follow in the same way and find that the paper contains 2, 5 cent pieces. One of them I put into the mysterious box, and thought I knew as much as any Yank . . .

We lunch, and then go on board the steamer . . . What a delicious feeling it is to glide down the . . . bay, under a cool awning, and in a lounge chair, with the sun shining on all the bustle of a crowded bay studded with sails and steamers & enclosed by high dark green hills. Wise is knocked up by over eating and I am not quite so well as I might be . . . I am sick before going to bed . . .

10 August

. . . We see a large family of porpoises coming towards the boat . . . They come close to the bow, and to our surprise swim at a tremendous pace, all in a heap, just a foot or so in front of the bow. The captain tells me that the porpoises frequently do this for the purpose of scratching their tails!! We see a turtle . . . Every single Yank, rich or poor, has his iced drink—generally iced laager beer. We have not touched wine since we left Liverpool. It is much too hot. Why is no shark forthcoming? . . . We are very comfortable. Whist & dozing occupies us.

11 August[1]

The pretty American girl who is on board with her blind father is very reserved, different from what we have heard about them! . . . What a difference there is between our small business men and the corresponding class of fellows over here. There are several on board, most gentlemanly and well-informed men, and without any of the bumptiousness of the British Army . . .

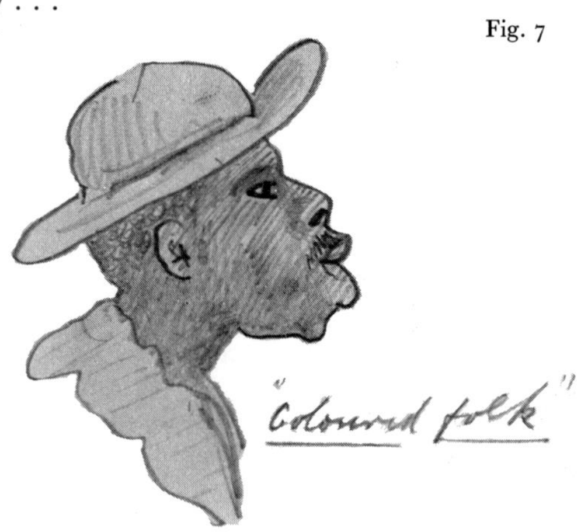

Fig. 7

Sketch in Maxse's diary

12 August

Coming on deck we find ourselves in the river & close to Savannah. At 9 a.m. we are on the wharf wh. is crowded with niggers, or as I must now call them "coloured folk", nigger being a term of contempt. Savannah swarms with these fellows (& not the best of them). They earn $1 a day for working on the landing stages when ships come up. It seems a great deal for doing next to nothing . . .

We put up at the Pulaski Hotel . . . We eat a capital dinner (soup of tommatoes and olives very good).

Wise and I took a strol round the city wh. is laid out in a series of squares. We were told that when the Indians made raids, the country people camped in these squares which were defended from the houses. Wise pays $7 (about £1.12.0)[2] to a man who carries us and our luggage about 500 yards!!

Our boat for Saint Simons Island started at 4 p.m. . . . What a beautiful journey . . . through narrow channels of water dividing the numerous

---

[1] Maxse began to confuse the dates. For example the Thursday and Friday of the voyage to Savannah were both noted as 10 August. He makes a similar mistake the following week, but eventually corrects himself. The dates given here have been corrected where necessary.

[2] Or, £1.60.

islands of the Georgian coast; in some places we were in narrow creeks between two well-wooded islands, at others on wide sheets of salt water with porpoises jumping about . . . We saw plenty of large birds, such as crane, heron, ganet . . . also porpoises, alligators & large fish. We passed but few houses in our journey . . .

13 August

I am awoke from my cramped-up little bunk by Wise who says that we have arrived at St. Simons I. It is about 5 a.m. and we are left on a wharf with all our baggage!

We enquire for Chapman's & find that he lives 8 miles off. Having put all our baggage into a store-house on the wharf we start off at a walk. We pass a mill and then come to a negro milking a cow. We ask him the way, & suggest that we shd. like some milk: he turns out to be a capital fellow, gives us water melons and milk and kills a chicken for our breakfast, wh. we do not eat. He then shows us the road and we tramp along at a good pace up a sandy wagon-track without any certainty of being received at Chapman's; he may not have either room or provisions for 4 hungry creatures. The sun comes out hot at about 8 & we march on in silence, stopping now and then for a man caught with the "grupe".[1] Bumf trees abound, but we don't get into any shade until we near Chapman's. We greatly prefer his part of the island. We see lots of game, and one big black snake. After being a whole fortnight on the sea I think this almost tropical vegetation quite delicious. The densely-growing underwood of palmeto and other green shrubs with the ilex trees covered over with hairy-fluffy moss is a pretty sight after many days of the "ever climbing wave".

At last we come to a thick wood, then an open field at the end of wh. we see a comparatively large house nestled in a clump of ilex. It is Chapman's, and we are not sorry. We don't know what our reception will be like as only one, Crutwell, is expected. We arrive at the door . . . That verandah with the basket chairs looks comfortable! We go into a little room . . . fitted up in English style and Mr. Chapman receives us very cordially indeed . . . He tells us that Mrs. Chapman has had a baby a week ago, and so we must be quiet. There are 2 rooms upstairs for us with 2 beds; there is a mattress on the floor and a couple of hammocks—much more than we had expected. There is a bath. How we enjoy that bath!! . . . Chapman gave us all clean shirts & we felt different beings.

Having eaten, we make an inspection of the crops—beans, peas, potatoes, cotton, corn, sugar cane, beet, cabbage, onions, rutabaga, turnips, asparagus, melons, tomatoes etc. . . . We have supper at about 7, and then a curious service composed chiefly of curious songs and dirges by the coloured people. I am getting very fond of the coloured men. At 9.30 to bed . . .

14 August

We are awoke at 5 a.m. by Mr. Chapman, given a cup of coffee and all set to work on a new kitchen wh. is to be built. Very hard work we find it, with the sweat pouring down our faces, & very hungry we are at 8 o'clock when we wash and have breakfast. Our food consists chiefly

---

[1] Presumably he means gripe.

of the food of the land: milk, potatoes, fish, honey, rice and any bird or beast that is shot. We find that we don't want any meat or wine . . .

15 August
. . . At 5 p.m. we start off on an exploring & shooting expedition . . . Chapman is a capital fellow—just the man for this sort of life. He treats the coloured people very well, is a perfect gentleman & has lots of go. The coloured people are devoted to him. I wish we could have been photographed as we left the house in the evening, with our large sun hats and varied handkerchiefs to keep off mosquitos. Most of us wore knickerbockers . . .

We enjoyed our walk through the beautiful woods with the chance of meeting rattlesnakes, deer, or wild boar, very much. We put up a covey of quail but did not bag any. Just as it was getting dark I brought down a large "fish-hawk" . . . at 60 yds . . . We walked a good distance in the dark, lighted by the brilliant fire-flies. We arrive at the small village of Hampton at 8.30 and walk into an old wooden house of Chapman's . . . A bathe in the river is proposed, and much to the horor of the natives we all plunge into the water without a thought of alligators or stinging fish . . .

16 August
Up early—4 a.m. breakfast—pack up eatables and proceed in two rudely-fashioned boats to the island "swarming with game".[1] Wise has Chapman's gun, Giles his rifle. Neither of them look quite at home. We get a few long shots at crane etc. as we go, also of a couple of porpoises. 2 miles down the river we come to a small wooden house, swarming with mosquitos and sand-flies . . . The island is well-wooded and wholly uninhabited except by birds and insects and snakes: in the winter there are swarms of duck.

Frank—a capital fellow, who reminds me of Adam Bede[2]—is our guide, and shouldering a most formidable weapon in the shape of a long musket of the time of The War, leads us through the entangled woods. I shoot several large birds of the crane kind . . . Wise shoots a water snake! Well done "Cracker" Wise.

We return, drink copiously of tea . . .

On our way back we have a great deal of excitement in chasing a porpoise up a narrow creek. With the certainty of being upset if the porpoise comes down the creek, our two boats are punted $\frac{1}{2}$ a mile up the creek—all six of us are ready to let the porpoise have it with guns, rifles, and even revolvers . . . After a long chase, with various exclamations of "he is coming" the porpoise escapes by a side creek . . . much to the happiness of our coloured friends who would much rather not have their boats smashed in by a lump of fat. They are very timid in facing this sea monster! We are disappointed in not seeing an alligator. I have seen the nose of one but not in time to shoot at him. We have a good meal at Hampton Pt. and return home at night in the ox-wagon— a nice jolting journey wh. prepares us for a good tea and bed.

17 August
. . . We work all day at the new saw pit. The weather is what we should call in England very hot, but it is by no means an enervating heat—one

---

[1] i.e. Little St. Simons Island.
[2] The novel *Adam Bede* by George Eliot had been published in England in 1859.

feels quite fit in spite of the pouring sweat. We are all reduced several pounds in flesh, but are none the worse for it. Giles is quite eaten up by every sort of insect. The mosquitos won't touch Wise—the "Cracker's" flesh is not even good enough for them! Flies, bugs, mosquitos, sand-flies, wood-ticks & other insects are the plague of our nights. There is plenty of game on the island, but it is all most impossible to get it. I have seen alligators, rattlesnakes, porpoises, ganet, crane, heron, buzzards, quail, doves, owles and many varied coloured small birds, and I hear there are turtle, otters, wild cats, deer, wild boar, and in the winter every kind of duck . . .

18 August
. . . Mrs. Chapman is well enough to sit out on the verandah with the baby. How much more comfortably things go when there is a woman to look after the household. I think that a man who emigrates *must* have a wife; his life becomes that of a mere animal unless he is married: but then, how much of his happiness depends upon the woman whom he has to live with in solitude! Chapman seems to have chosen very well. The baby is very ugly, as of course all babies always are, and its mother is sensible enough not to call it pretty. It has arrived 6 weeks before it was expected, and perhaps that accounts for its goodness in the squeaking line—it never cries! Thank goodness for that! We are very lucky in these things—fancy if we four had to join in a chorus of praise of an ugly babe who always squawled!

19 August
Wise and self get up at 4 a.m. and start on a camping-out expedition to Hampton Point. Guided by a "sportsman" . . . & accompanied with 3 dogs we start as the sun rises. These sun rises are very rapid: night is changed into day in 10 minutes. Wise, eager for a cannonade at a sitting sparrow, marches contentedly on with both gun & rifle . . . hoping for a lion round every bush . . . Our coloured guide makes his way through the thick underwood with a gay heart and little thinks of the fears he is causing in my timid breast as he ballances his 2 yard barrel nicely on his shoulder with its muzzle pointed at my head . . .

In the afternoon I go out alone in a boat with Frank, the most simpleminded & best fellow imaginable. I have a long talk with him about slavery and the effect of freedom on the coloured people: it is only on hearing of the horrors inflicted upon slaves from the mouth of a man who has been one, and of the great benefits that have arisen from freedom, that one can understand the difference between the past and the present state of the negro world. I shall never forget that long talk . . . with the tall, handsome-looking man, who is the owner of a small house & [a] few acres of land wh. he cultivates, & of a family of wh. he is very fond, having commenced life and lived for 14 years under the whip of the slave driver. I should like to have taken down the simple words of this straightforward man as he told me his storey. His honesty and simplicity, coupled with his straightforward intelligence, reminds me of Adam Bede . . . He has the build, the cares and the same simple-hearted religion as George Eliot['s] hero . . .

27 August
. . . In the evening I kill my first alligator—one about 4½ feet long. I skin him immediately and hope to preserve his skin. He is very hard to

kill. He has a bullet through his head, his brains are half out, he is half skinned and yet he is alive . . .

6 September

. . . We all receive a heavy shock in the shape of a telegram from my father saying that I am to return at once as I am gazetted to "a" regiment. I wished he had said what regiment . . . We must start tomorrow.'

Their return journey took them by steamer to Brunswick and thence by train to Savannah, Richmond and Washington through to New York.

'*11 September*

. . . We drive to the 5th Avenue Hotel—one of the best in N.Y. Have a bath, dress like decent people again and eat a good breakfast . . .

We meet Oscar Wilde[1] in the hall of our hotel—dressed in a fantastic costume & with flowing hair. Wise knows him a little, and introduces himself and me. Oscar's manner is very pleasant: he asks both to his box at the theatre tonight, and we ask him to dine with us . . .

. . . of course the great Oscar is late. At last he comes, followed by a crowd of wondering people. His evening dress is not so peculiar as might be expected.

He is very interesting at dinner, & often amusing. He talks very well, but monopolises all the conversation. His stories are good & well told, in spite of his affectations.

There is a great deal more in him than I had thought. At the play he is the centre of attraction. The audience applaud whenever they catch a glimpse of him.

The house is a large one and is quite full; but the effect is spoiled by the dress of the audience—all of whom are in their morning clothes. We are the only people in evening dress in the place . . .

We are obliged to walk home in the pouring rain as no cabs are about. In fact the New York cabmen are very independent people. They charge exhorbitant prices—3 dollars (13s)[2]—for a short drive—and never stay out late at night.

Oscar Wilde asks us to breakfast tomorrow . . .

12 September

Wilde after breakfast, wh. is only over at 1 p.m., takes us to a beautiful jewellers . . .'

Later that afternoon they sailed from New York in the *Alaska* and two days out Maxse discontinued the diary.[3]

Maxse Papers 347–348.

---

[1] Oscar Wilde (1856–1900), the wit and dramatist, was on a tour of the United States lecturing on aesthetics.

[2] Or, 65p.

[3] On returning to England Maxse joined the 7th Fusiliers, the beginning of a most distinguished military career in which he saw service in India, the Sudan, the Boer War and the 1914–1918 War. Between 1919 and 1923 he was G.O.C. in Chief, Northern Command, England. He died in 1958. George Meredith's novel *Beauchamp's Career* (1876) is said to be largely a character study of his father, Frederick Augustus Maxse.

Appendix: Sussex and America

The numerous links between Sussex and America have been explored in a series of articles by David McLean published in volumes four and five of the now defunct *Sussex County Magazine* in 1930 and 1931. Throughout the following list the *Sussex County Magazine* articles referred to form part of this well illustrated series which was entitled 'Sussex and the U.S.A.'. These volumes are available for reference at the West Sussex Record Office at Chichester or through all principal libraries throughout the county.

Ardingly, near Haywards Heath

A replica of Wakehurst Place, an Elizabethan mansion built by Sir Edward Culpeper in 1590, was built at Newport, Rhode Island, in 1884. There is a brief description of the Newport counterpart by Gerald W. E. Loder in *Wakehurst Place, Sussex* (1907), p. 120, with two photographic views. Part of the grounds of the Ardingly Wakehurst Place, but not the house itself, are open to the public. There are some fine brasses to commemorate the Culpeper family in Ardingly parish church.

From one of the Kent branches of the Culpeper family (who lived at Leeds Castle, near Maidstone) came Thomas, 2nd Lord Culpeper (1635–1689) who was commissioned Governor of Virginia in 1675. For an account of his American career see *Sussex County Magazine*, vol. 5, pp. 24–30.

Bexhill, Boxgrove, Broadwater and Withyham

Thomas West, 3rd Baron De La Warr (1577–1618) was appointed the first Governor of Virginia in 1609. The State, Bay and River are all named after him. Although born in Hampshire (at Wherwell) he had many Sussex connections as may be seen in the De La Warr monuments in Boxgrove Priory (near Chichester) and the parish churches of Broadwater (near Worthing) and Withyham (near East Grinstead). Their later connection with Bexhill is commemorated in the De La Warr Pavilion on the seafront. De La Warr made a further Sussex link through his marriage to Cecily, daughter of Sir Thomas Shirley of Wiston. Although the Elizabethan Wiston House is not open to the public it may be viewed from the driveway leading to the church next door. (William Shirley, who came from this same Sussex family, became Governor of Massachusetts in the mid-18th century, see below.) For a two-part article on the De La Warr connection with Sussex see *Sussex County Magazine*, vol. 4, pp. 791–795, 839–842.

Chichester

Peter Pelham (*c*.1695–1751), artist and engraver of Boston, is said to have emigrated from Chichester in 1726. He is reputed to be the engraver of the first mezzotint plate prepared in America. His son, Henry, made a survey of the military fortifications at Charlestown, soon after the battle of Bunker Hill. General Gage (see under Firle, below) refused him permission to publish this on account of the military detail disclosed. The plan, however, was eventually incorporated in a larger map of Boston and surrounding countryside which Pelham published two years later in

1777. There is an original copy of Pelham's map in the West Sussex Record Office, West Dean MS. 3190. For a reference to this map see above, p. 20. For a brief study of Pelham and his family see *Sussex County Magazine*, vol. 5, pp. 674–679.

Dame Agnes Frankland, formerly of Massachusetts, came to live and be buried in Chichester in the late 18th century. Born in the small fishing village of Marblehead, Massachusetts, in 1726, she was a servant girl, of poor parents, who fell in love with a wealthy young Englishman, Charles Henry Frankland. Their fairy-tale romance has inspired at least five novels and the poem *Agnes* by Oliver Wendell Holmes. They lived in Boston, at the centre of fashionable society, with a country residence at Hopkinton. After his death she eventually came to live in England where she settled in Chichester in 1777, living at 5 West Pallant (not open to the public, but may be seen from the outside). She then remarried in 1781 and lived in Little London in the parish of St. Andrew Oxmarket. For the record of her marriage to John Drew of Chichester see the register of All Saints in the Pallant, Chichester (West Sussex Record Office, Par. 36/1/1/3). The baptisms and burials register for the same parish (Par. 36/1/1/2) records the baptism of 'Cato Cromwell, a Negro Boy of Lady Frankland's from Boston in America . . .' on 3 April 1775, and his burial on 12 April 1776. Dame Agnes herself was buried in the Litten graveyard in St. Pancras. The memorial stone still survives near the roadway in New Park Road, Chichester. For further details see the monograph by Stella Palmer, *Dame Agnes Frankland, 1726–1783, and Some Chichester Contemporaries* (Chichester Paper no. 45, 1964).

The Royal Sussex Regiment fought in some of the major engagements of the American War of Independence, including Bunker Hill, Brooklyn and White Plains. The regimental museum is housed in the Chichester City Museum in Little London.

Henry Hore, who became the manager of the Chichester branch of the Capital & Counties Bank in East Street in the 1880s, fought with the Federal army in the Civil War. Part of a letter written to his cousin Olivia from Fredericksburg, Virginia, dated 1 May 1863, is transcribed by Bernard Price in his *Sussex: People, Places, Things* (1975), pp. 145–154.

Coolham, near Billingshurst

William Penn, the founder of Pennsylvania, lived at nearby Warming-hurst (see below) and was a worshipper at the Blue Idol Meeting House.

His daughter Laetitia ('Tishe') who died in 1746 is buried here. The Blue Idol may be visited. There are various mementoes relating to Penn on display, and a brief guide is available.

Edburton, near Hurstpierpoint

A former rector of Edburton, the Reverend George Keith (*c.*1638–1716), became the first missionary in North America for the Society for the Propagation of the Gospel in Foreign Parts. A mathematical scholar and Quaker, he first went to America in 1684 where he was appointed Surveyor-General of New Jersey to map the boundary line between New Jersey and New York. In 1689 he settled in Philadelphia where he became headmaster of the Quaker school founded by William Penn. He eventually split with the Quakers and after returning to England was ordained as a Church of England clergyman in 1700. In 1702 he returned to America under the auspices of the S.P.G. where he did much to expand the church in New Jersey and throughout his travels which took him between Massachusetts and North Carolina. After his return to England he was appointed to the living at Edburton in 1705 where he remained until his death in 1716.

There are two memorials to George Keith at Edburton church. On the south side of the nave, near the pulpit, a memorial window shows the original S.P.G. seal and records that Keith, as their first missionary, sailed to America in the Admiralty ship *Centurion* in 1702. In the churchyard, between the north transept and a spreading yew, is a table tomb which replaces an earlier monument and bears the following inscription on the top:

Sacred to the Memory
of The Reverend
GEORGE KEITH
Missionary of the Society
for the Propagation of the
Gospel to the American
Colonies 1702–1704
This Stone is placed
here in the year 1932
by the Dioceses of the
American Church which
include the Places he visited
MASSACHUSETTS
CONNECTICUT
RHODE ISLAND   LONG ISLAND
NEW YORK   NEW JERSEY
NEWARK   PENNSYLVANIA
VIRGINIA   SOUTHERN VIRGINIA
EAST CAROLINA
His work is remembered
His memory is honoured

A short biography of George Keith may be purchased in the church.

Felpham, near Bognor Regis

William Blake (1757–1827) the poet, visionary and painter who wrote and illustrated *America* in 1793 came to live at Felpham a few years later. Blake regarded America as the land of freedom and here he tells, in allegorical form, the story of the struggle for American independence. The text is illustrated by hand-coloured drawings representing some of Blake's most splendid work. A very fine coloured facsimile is held by the West Sussex Record Office; Crookshank Collection no. 154. Blake's cottage at Felpham (near *The Fox* inn) is not open to the public. It is marked by a wall-plaque and may be seen from the road.

Firle, near Lewes

General Thomas Gage (1721–1787) of Firle Place succeeded Sir Jeffrey Amherst as Governor-General in North America in 1763. In 1774 he was appointed Governor-in-Chief and Captain-General of Massachusetts where he was responsible for carrying out British policy at the outbreak of the War of Independence. He ordered troops to Lexington and Concord and was in overall command of the British attack on Bunker Hill. There are portraits of him and documents relating to his North American service on display at Firle Place which is open to the public. The Gage family tombs are in St. Peter's church at Firle. See *Sussex County Magazine* vol. 5, pp. 354–361, 401–405.

Goodwood, near Chichester

Charles Lennox, 2nd Duke of Richmond (1701–1750, a grandson of King Charles II), who lived at Goodwood House, did much to beautify and improve its surrounding parkland. He was a leading patron of botanical expeditions to North America in search of plants. Many specimens were sent from North America to Goodwood by John Bartram through a London agent, Peter Collinson. See Josephine Herbst, *New Green World* (1954). For some letters from Collinson to the Duke, in which he refers to trade with New York and Philadelphia, see the West Sussex Record Office, Goodwood MS. 108, ff. 793–799.

The Duke's son, the 3rd Duke of Richmond (1734/5–1806), took a leading part in American affairs in the House of Lords during the War of Independence. See above, pp. 15, 22–23.

Goodwood House is open to the public.

Hailsham, near Eastbourne

In the parish church of St. Mary's is a memorial with the following inscription:

In / Memory of / Colonel Philip / Van Cortlandt / of the Manor of / Cortlandt / A Retired Royalist / officer / of the American War. / Died at Hailsham / May 1814 / Aged 74 years. / The Memory of the Just / is blessed. Prov. X. VII.

South Harting, near Petersfield

Uppark, built *c.*1685–1690, was the home of Sir Matthew Fetherstonhaugh, a wealthy 18th century Member of Parliament. With several leading politicians he became involved with the Grand Ohio Company, a speculative venture established in 1769 to finance the setting-up of an American settlement to be called Vandalia, in what is now West Virginia. Fetherstonhaugh commissioned Henry Keene to erect a monument to the scheme in the form of a Gothic tower in the grounds of Uppark. The ruins of the Vandalian Tower still survive on the Downs overlooking Harting. Close to Harting Hill, it may be seen from several surrounding viewpoints. The house is open to the public. See Margaret Meade-Fetherstonhaugh & Oliver Warner, *Uppark and its People* (1964). In the West Sussex Record Office there is a microfilm copy (M.F. 24) of original documents relating to this scheme.

Hastings

Herbert Pelham (1600–1673), who lived for a time in Hastings, joined the Massachusetts Company in 1629. He emigrated to New England soon after, where he took an active part in local affairs. He became the first treasurer of Harvard College in 1643. In 1646 he was one of the commissioners for arranging a treaty with the Narrangansett and Niantic

Indians. For an illustration of his house at Hastings and an article about his life see *Sussex County Magazine*, vol. 4, pp. 357–369.

Part of Hastings seafront was once a derelict wasteland where squatters built shacks and shanties in much the same way as many of the early Americans built whatever and wherever they pleased. Reflecting their view of pioneer America, Hastings people came to call this wasteland the America Ground. In the mid-19th century it was appropriated by the Crown and re-developed to form the area now covered by Harold Place, Robertson Terrace, Robertson Street, Carlisle Parade, Trinity Street and Claremont.

Haywards Heath and Lindfield

Under the guiding influence of the Quaker philanthropist William Allen, an allotment colony was established in the 19th century between Haywards Heath and Lindfield. Small cottages with their own land attached were made available to help the poor. The settlement became known as America, another example, as at Hastings, of how local people considered America was being settled. When the area was redeveloped in the present century the local roads were given American names to per-petuate the memory of the colony, such as America Lane, New England Road, Penn Crescent, Washington Road. See Helena Hall, *William Allen, 1770–1843* (1953), pp. 116–123.

Heathfield

The Reverend Robert Hunt (*c.*1568–1608), vicar of Heathfield from 1602, was appointed chaplain to the English expedition which sailed for Virginia in December 1606 to found Jamestown in 1607. He became the first minister to establish the Protestant church in the American colonies. A bronze bas-relief showing him celebrating the first communion at Jamestown in June 1607 was erected at Jamestown in 1922. For a photo-graph of this memorial and an article about Hunt see *Sussex County Magazine*, vol. 4, pp. 981–987.

Heyshott, near Midhurst

Richard Cobden, M.P., one of the most noted politicians to forge Anglo-American understanding in the 19th century, had his home at Dunford House, Heyshott. From here he conducted a vast and influential corres-pondence with America, especially at the time of the Civil War (see above, pp. 65–76). Dunford House, which today is a conference centre run by the Young Men's Christian Association, may be visited by serious students, strictly by appointment only with the Principal. There are many relics of Cobden's life preserved here, including part of his library. His grave is in nearby West Lavington churchyard. There is also a sandstone obelisk to his memory (just off the lane leading from the A.286 to Pendean sandpit, north-west of Dunford) inscribed with Cobden's name and dates and the words

FREE TRADE

PEACE GOODWILL

AMONG NATIONS

Lewes

Tom Paine (1737–1809), one of the founders of American independence, lived at Bull House, High Street, Lewes, between 1768 and 1774. He was stationed at Lewes as an excise officer. Through Benjamin Franklin's advice, Paine went to Philadelphia in 1774 where he became one of the leading propagandists for the American cause, notably through his *Common Sense* (1776) in which he advocated separation from Britain. Its publication had an immediate and profound effect in stirring up support for the American cause and the Declaration of Independence. See Eric Foner, *Tom Paine and Revolutionary America* (1976). Bull House is owned by the Sussex Archaeological Trust and is open to the public as a restaurant. For two articles about Paine's life, including his Lewes connections, see *Sussex County Magazine*, vol. 4, pp. 184–190, 293–301.

Delaware Road, Lewes, was named by the Mayor of Lewes from the State of Delaware in 1964 to commemorate his visit to the town.

Petworth

George Percy (1580–1632), son of the 8th Earl of Northumberland who lived at Petworth House, was one of the original adventurers who sailed to Virginia in the first expedition of James I's reign in December 1606. His expedition established the first permanent English settlement in North America. He was one of the founders of the second Company of Virginia in 1609, was a member of the Council of Virginia and was twice appointed Deputy-Governor of the colony between 1609 and 1612. He took a leading part in the bitter power struggles that threatened to destroy the very existence of the early colony, and after his return to England composed his own personal view of the events as he himself had seen them in a manuscript which he entitled 'A Trewe Relatyon of the Proceedings and Occurrentes of Momente which have Happened in Virginia, from . . . 1609, untill . . . 1612'. The original manuscript was preserved at Petworth House until it was sold to an American dealer for £6,600 in 1928.[1] A manuscript copy of the original has been retained amongst the Petworth House Archives. Petworth House is open to the public.[2] For an article on George Percy see *Sussex County Magazine*, vol. 4, pp. 602–608, 650–654.

One of the English branches of the Washington family, from which George Washington, first President of the United States, was descended, was living in Petworth in the late 17th century. For this connection see *Sussex County Magazine*, vol. 4, pp. 47–58. There are references to several members of the Washington family in the Petworth parish register which is in the West Sussex Record Office, Par. 149/1/1/1. For another Washington connection with Sussex see under Staplefield, below.

Preston, near Brighton

William Shirley (1694–1771), Governor of Massachusetts from 1741 to 1757, was born at Preston. Preston Manor, one of the ancestral seats of the Shirley family, is open to the public. A barrister, William Shirley emigrated to New England in 1731 where he became a noted place-hunter. As Governor he was chiefly noted for his strenuous opposition to

---

[1] A copy of the Sotheby's sale catalogue which includes details of many very important items of early American interest is held by the West Sussex Record Office, library no. 2584.
[2] Note that the Petworth House Archives are *not* available for inspection at Petworth House. They may be seen, by prior appointment, at the West Sussex Record Office.

the French in North America and his offensive operations against Canada.
See *Sussex County Magazine*, vol. 5, pp. 199–205, 268–272. There is a
further article by another author, Isabel Haddan, entitled 'William
Shirley and Some of his Descendants' in the same volume, pp. 273–277.

Ringmer and South Malling, near Lewes

The village sign by the side of the main road records that the wives of
both John Harvard and William Penn were from Ringmer. John Harvard
(1607–1638), who left money and books in his will for the founding of
Harvard College, Cambridge, Massachusetts, and after whom the
College was named, married Anne Sadler, daughter of the rector of
Ringmer. Their marriage took place at St. Michael's church, South
Malling in 1636 and is recorded in the parish register. (This register is
retained by the incumbent.) William Penn's first wife, Guilelma Maria
Springett, was the daughter of Sir William Springett of Broyle Place,
Ringmer (not open to the public). Memorials to both Harvard's and
Penn's fathers-in-law are in Ringmer parish church. The village sign
also shows a picture of Timothy the tortoise which belonged to the 18th
century naturalist, Gilbert White. Timothy was said to have been an
American tortoise born in Virginia, and was bought by White's uncle
(who lived in Ringmer) from a sailor in Chichester. See Sylvia Townsend
Warner, *The Portrait of a Tortoise* . . . (1946), p. 11.

Rottingdean, near Brighton

When the cemetery at Forest Lawns, San Francisco, was being laid out,
an offer was made to purchase the medieval parish church of St. Margaret
at Rottingdean and re-erect it stone by stone in California. The offer
being refused (!) a replica was built instead, and dedicated as the Church
of the Recessional, after Rudyard Kipling's poem.

Kipling lived at the Elms, Rottingdean, from 1897 to 1902 (not open
to the public) where he wrote *Recessional* to celebrate Queen Victoria's
Diamond Jubilee. Its publication was due to one of his American friends,
Sallie Norton. She saw him throw it into the waste-paper basket, rescued
it and persuaded him to publish.

Rye

The Reverend John Allin, Puritan vicar of Rye from 1653 to 1662, was
one of the earliest Harvard graduates in 1643. In 1662 he was ejected
from Rye as a Puritan. In later life he returned to America where he
became minister at Woodbridge, New Jersey, in the 1680s. See *Sussex
County Magazine*, vol. 5, pp. 822–826.

The township of Rye in New York State was founded in the 17th century
by settlers from Rye, Sussex. Both parishes observe the second Sunday in
Advent as an annual day of commemoration.

Lamb House in West Street was formerly the home of the American
born novelist Henry James (1843–1916) who lived here between 1897
and 1916. In 1950 the widow of his heir and nephew, Henry James
Junior of New York City, presented Lamb House to the National Trust
'to be preserved as an enduring symbol of the ties that unite the British
and American people'. The house is open to the public. See *Sussex County
Magazine*, vol. 5, pp. 758–762, and H. Montgomery Hyde, *The Story of
Lamb House, Rye, The Home of Henry James* (1966).

Staplefield, near Haywards Heath

Tyes was the home of Margaret Butler who married Lawrence Washington in 1588. Their grandson, John Washington, emigrated to Virginia, and his grandson was George Washington, first President of the United States. The house at Staplefield is not open to the public. See *Sussex County Magazine*, vol. 4, pp. 47–58.

Steyning

The former Quaker Meeting House in Steyning commemorates William Penn's close associations with local Friends' meetings. Divided into two private homes, one part is called Penn's House, and the smaller, Penn's Cottage. The brick, stone and tiled building may be seen from the Horsham Road on the western edge of the town. The south end bears a wall-plaque with the inscription:

QUAKER

MEETING HOUSE

1678

In *Some Records of the Early Friends in Surrey and Sussex* ... (1886), Thomas W. Marsh recalls the (unproven) tradition that timbers from the ship *Welcome* in which Penn sailed to America in 1682 were later incorporated into the building (p. 37). The story of 'The Old Meeting House, Steyning' is told by the Rev. H. E. B. Arnold in *Sussex County Magazine*, vol. 6 (1932), pp. 500–504. For other references to Penn and Sussex see under Coolham, Ringmer and Warminghurst.

Warminghurst, near Horsham

William Penn, the Quaker founder of Pennsylvania, had his home at Warminghurst Place in the late 17th century. It was here that he drafted the first constitution of Pennsylvania. He also held Quaker meetings here. When he returned to England in 1684 to sort out a boundary dispute over the boundary with Maryland, the magistrates at the Court of Quarter Sessions held at Arundel, Sussex, in January 1684/5, ordered that he be apprehended for permitting such meetings at his house. The legal presentment, which is in the West Sussex Record Office (QR/W173, m. 31), laid the charge that

> 'William Penn . . . Gent, as a factious and seditious person . . . doth frequently entertaine and keepe unlawfull assembley & Conventicles in his dwelling House . . . usualy . . . assembled to ye number of one or two hundred . . . and sometimes moore to the terrer of ye Kings Leige people & in Contempt of ye King & his Lawes . . .'

The house, which stood to the south of Warminghurst church, was demolished in the 18th century for the erection of a new house in its place. There is a small illustration of Warminghurst Place on a map of Warminghurst of 1707 in the British Museum (Add. MS. 37,420), a copy of which is in the West Sussex Record Office (Add. MS. 2,155), and which is also reproduced in the church guide. For other Sussex connections with William Penn see under Coolham, Ringmer and Steyning, above. See also *Sussex County Magazine*, vol. 4, pp. 125–135, and Thomas W. Marsh, *Some Records of the Early Friends in Surrey and Sussex* ... (1886).

*   *   *   *   *   *   *

Further links between Sussex and America were forged by emigrants who naturally took with them the customs, manners and speech of their homeland. In the first place many of the pioneers named their new settlements with obvious nostalgia, so that peppered across the United States are literally scores of place-names transplanted from England. From Sussex, for example, are Arundel Village (Maryland), Horsham (Pennsylvania), Lewes (Delaware), Shoreham (Vermont) and Rye (New York). Between Maryland and Colorado there are at least ten places called Brighton, and two, New Brighton (Minnesota and Pennsylvania). Between New York and Nebraska there are at least eight townships named after yet another Sussex coastal town, Hastings. Then the name of Sussex itself has been given to settlements in New Jersey, Virginia, Wisconsin and Wyoming, and to three counties in Delaware, New Jersey and Virginia.

Workaday traditions and habits were also transplanted in America— albeit in a far less self-conscious fashion—as in speech and methods of craftsmanship.

The English language taken over by the early settlers became so deeply rooted in the American tradition that modern American English still actively preserves certain forms of archaic English. Words such as 'hog', 'gotten' and 'fall', familiar enough in America today, were once commonly heard in England. 'Examination of the literature and the documentary records of seventeenth- and eighteenth-century America discloses a good many dialect words and therefore, from the point of view of English writers, unworthy to be used in literature. Some of these words, brought over here in the seventeenth and eighteenth centuries and recorded by men who were not primarily writers, have been preserved in American English.'[1] In the preface to his *Dictionary of the Sussex Dialect and Collection of Provincialisms in use in the County of Sussex* of 1875 the Reverend W. D. Parish could deplore the use of new words 'to the exclusion of many good old English words which are to this day more frequently used in the United States of America than in our own country'. And even in pronunciation Professor Eilert Ekwall concludes that 'educated American pronunciation on the whole remains at the stage which British pronunciation had reached about the time of the Revolution, while modern British pronunciation has left that stage far behind'.[2]

Turning specifically to Sussex, R. Thurston Hopkins has noted some of the observations of Louis J. Jennings who wrote of Sussex Americanisms in 1884: 'My Etchingham friend frequently made use of the expression "I reckon", so that, but for his misplaced h's—and he dropped them all over the road in a most reckless and amazing manner—he might have been a Southern or Western American. He also used the word "Fall", in speaking of the autumn. I am told that most hard-winged insects are commonly called "bugs" as in America; thus we hear of the ladybug (lady-bird), the May-bug (cockchafer), the June-bug (the green beetle), and so forth. I have heard the word "axey" for ague in the Eastern States, just as it is used to this hour in many parts of Sussex.'[3]

Yet another link is the Sussex dialect poem of *Jan Cladpole's Trip to 'Merricur in Search of Dollar Trees* by Richard Lower, a 19th century Sussex schoolmaster.[4]

---

[1] Thomas Pyles, *Words and Ways of American English* (1954), p. 23.
[2] Quoted in Pyles, *op. cit.*, p. 56.
[3] Quoted in *Sussex Pilgrimages* (1st edn. 1927), p. 99.
[4] There is a copy of the poem in the West Sussex Record Office, Crookshank Collection no. 413.

There are also a great many similarities between certain forms of English and American domestic architecture, as the early colonial settlers quite naturally took their traditional building practices with them. Indeed, for a time at least, 'the vernacular architecture of North America [may be] considered as a regional variation of English vernacular'. In the northern half of the colonies the settlers 'brought over the plan types to which they had been accustomed; one room deep, two storeys in height, central chimneys placed back to back, and the corresponding structural forms, box-frame of heavy timber sections, light studded wall and independent roof construction . . .' In the southern half of the colonies there is far less vernacular, but of these 'many preserve a plan one room in depth but with gable chimneys,[1] and some retain the projecting porch and staircase common throughout England at the turn of the 17c. Although most homes were timber-framed, a good proportion of the surviving examples are of brick with similar elaboration of chimney stack and gable wall to contemporary work in Eastern and South Eastern England.'[2]

In his study of Connecticut houses, J. Frederick Kelly has identified several proofs that the early settlers were working for some time in an English idiom as in their 'universal and persistent' use of oak. 'That the colonists, with abundance of other woods, both hard and soft, at their disposal, should have chosen oak, means simply that they elected to use the one material with the working of which they were already most familiar, and the physical properties of which they most perfectly understood . . . In many other ways, too, the influence of the mother country is to be seen reflected in the early Connecticut houses. Examples are the comparatively low height of story; the close proximity of the first floor to the ground; the steepness of pitch of the early roofs; and the large size of the chimney stack in relation to the general plan . . .'[3]

These building traditions taken over to America were deep-rooted in centuries of usage in South-Eastern and Eastern England. Its development in Sussex is traced by R. T. Mason in his *Framed Buildings of the Weald* (2nd edn. 1969). Several timber-framed buildings are preserved at the Open Air Museum at Singleton, near Chichester. What is quite clear is that there is still much research waiting to be done to investigate the relationship between the timber-framed houses of England and America in the light of the advanced studies into vernacular architecture being undertaken in England at the present time, such as by the Open Air Museum and the Wealden Buildings Study Group.

The connection does not necessarily end with the wooden buildings of the early colonists, for during the first half of the 19th century there was a possible link between the beach-flint buildings of Sussex and the cobblestone buildings of the Lake Ontario Plain of western New York. The connection has been researched by Robert W. Frasch of the Rochester Museum of Arts and Sciences, New York. There are copies of his notes including 'Flint Buildings in Sussex—a Traveller's Notebook Data collected by Robert W. Frasch in the South Downs and along the Sussex

---

[1] There is a series of photographs comparing a gable-end chimney at Sedlescombe, near Hastings, with three examples in Virginia in the article 'An American's Impressions' by Delos H. Smith, an American architect, in *Sussex County Magazine*, vol. 5 (1931), pp. 364–368.
[2] R. W. Brunskill, *Illustrated Handbook of Vernacular Architecture* (1971), pp. 184–189.
[3] J. Frederick Kelly, *Early Domestic Architecture of Connecticut* (2nd impn. 1963), pp. 3–4.

Coast from Chichester to Hastings in September, 1970' in the West Sussex Record Office (M.P. 1218).

The craft of using smoothly-shaped cobblestones for building walls seems to have started quite suddenly south of Rochester in about 1825. As a building style it was without precedent in America and it has been suggested that the fashion might have been introduced by a Sussex emigrant, as exact parallels have been observed in certain Sussex buildings. There is, however, no evidence to prove that this was actually the case, and much more research, particularly documentary, remains to be carried out.

Mr. Frasch's report identifies the following Sussex buildings of particular significance in establishing the link:

Chichester

The *Richmond Arms* on Stockbridge Road is now one of the few surviving examples of a group of flint buildings surrounding the canal basin which developed around the canal which opened in 1823. 'This group is an interesting historical parallel with New York State cobblestone buildings that were built along the route of the Erie Canal in the 1830s and 1840s.'

Worthing

Nos. 1, 16 and 18[1] Prospect Place, c.1800–1810. 'The masonry is the same as American cobblestone work.'

West Tarring, now a suburb of Worthing

Nos. 54 and 56[2] Church Road. 'Englishmen seeking an exact duplicate of the most typical American cobblestone masonry mortar treatment can find it on this house. Coursed beach-flints are used with mortar shaped into raised triangles between each stone and into a raised ridge between rows of stones.'

Brighton

'The Brighton beach-flint masonry bears a closer resemblance to American cobblestone masonry than any other in England . . .'

No. 33 Marlborough Place. 'A charming small two-story row house of untarred beach-flints and fine mortar treatment identical to New York cobblestone masonry.'

Rottingdean, near Brighton

' "Tallboys" High Street . . . is coursed beach-flint with masonry treatment identical to American cobblestone masonry. A sign is dated 1780 on the storefront.'

Ovingdean, near Brighton

The Rectory, curate's house and coach house, built c.1804–1807, 'are proof positive that Sussex masons built exact prototypes of American cobblestone masonry (1825–1860) at least three decades earlier in 1804'.

[1] and the adjoining no. 14, appropriately called *Cobbles* (ed.).
[2] and the adjoining no. 58 (ed.).

Index

Adam Bede, by George Eliot (1859), 94, 95
Agricultural Revolution (in Great Britain), 32
Agriculture in U.S.A., 45–47, 80, 81, 90
Alabama, 54, 57
Alabama incident, 1862, 66
Alaska, S.S., 96
Albany, N.Y., 41, 81
Albion, H.M.S., 26, 28
Aldingbourne, Sussex, 33–34, 37, 42, 43
Allegheny Mts., 55, 79, 81
Allen, William, 101
Allibone, S. Austin, 57
Allin, Rev. John, v, 103
America, by William Blake (1793), 99
America, 'colony' in Sussex, 101
America Ground, Hastings, Sussex, 101
America and Sussex, 97–107
American Anti-Slavery Society, 51, 52
American Diaries of Richard Cobden, The, ed. Elizabeth Hoon Cawley (1952), 77
American Notes, by Charles Dickens (1842), 77, 85, 86, 87
American War of Independence, v, 15, 17–23, 98, 99, 100
Americans in England: American Indians, 11–13; Cromwell, Cato, 98; Frankland, Dame Agnes, 98; James, Henry, v, 103; Lewes, Mayor of, Del., 102; Timothy the tortoise, 103
Amherst, Sir Jeffrey, 9, 10, 99
Anabaptists, 14
Anderson, Major Robert, 63–65
Andersonville Prison, Ga., 75
Appleton, Henry, 32
Appomattox, Va., 76
Archibald, E., 49
Architecture, vernacular, in England and America, 106
Ardingly, Sussex, 97
Arizona, 45
Arkansas, 54, 57, 67
Arnold, Matthew, and *Civilisation in the United States . . .* (1888), 77
Arthur, James, 34
Arundel, Sussex, vi, 104
Arundel Castle, Sussex, 56
Arundel Village, Md., 105
Aspinwall, W. H., 74
Atchison, Topeka & Sante Fe Rail Road Company, 45
Atkinson, William, 43–45
Attlee, R., 34
Attree, John, 37
Auburn State Prison, N.Y., 85
Augusta, Fort, Pa., 9

Badcock, Captain William Stanhope, 26–31
Badcock Papers, 26–31
Baltimore, Md., 29, 30, 44, 59, 78, 79
Barbados, 14

Barnard, John, 40
Barney, Commodore ——, 26
Barrie, Captain Robert, 29, 30
Bartram, John, 100
Bayley, William, 34
Beauregard, General P. G. T., 63
Benedict, Md., 26, 27, 28, 29
Bermuda, 26, 28
Bexhill, Sussex, 97
Blake, William, and *America* (1793), 99
Bloomfield, Thomas, 45
Blue Idol Meeting House, Coolham, Sussex, 98
Boardman, Judge, 78
Boniface, Edmund, 34
Boone, Thomas, 13
Boston, Mass., 17, 18, 19, 20, 23, 49, 51, 57, 62, 70, 75, 76, 82, 83, 85, 90, 97, 98
Boston Courier, 57
Botanical expeditions to North America, 100
Boxgrove, Sussex, 97
Bradford, J. D., 76
Bridger, Thomas, 34
Bright, John, 66
Brighton, 107; as U.S.A. place name, 105
Bristol, England, 18
Bristow, John, 36
Britannia, sailing packet, 83
British Museum Additional Manuscripts, 66, 69, 77, 83, 90, 104
British Protective Emigrant Society, 47
Broadwater, Sussex, 97
Brooklyn, N.Y., 3, 57, 78, 98
Brougham, Henry, 55
Brown, John, 58, 61, 62, 71
Brownsville, Pa., 80
Brune, H.M.S., 26, 29, 30
Brunskill, R. W., and *Illustrated Handbook of Vernacular Architecture* (1971), 106
Bryce, James, and *The American Commonwealth* (1888), 77
Buckle, Rear-Admiral C. M., 77
Buffalo, N.Y., 81, 90
Bunch, Robert, 61–65
Bunker Hill, Battle of, 19–20, 97, 98, 100
Burdett, Sir Francis, 76
Burgess, John, 43
Burgoyne, General John, 23
Burke, Edmund, 23
Burnand, John, 34
Burrell, Sir Charles Merrick, 35–36
Butcher, Mrs. ——, 40
Butcher, Richard, 40
Butler, Margaret, 104

Cabet, Etienne, 44
Caffin, Mathew, 35
Caird, James, 69, 90
Cairo, Ill., 85–86, 90
California, v, 5, 103
Cambridge, Mass., 20, 103

Campbell, John, 4th Earl of Loudon, 7
Canada, 6, 7, 15, 26, 41, 53, 81–82, 90, 103
Canada, S.S., 85
Canning, George, 72
Capital & Counties Bank, Chichester, 98
Carlin, Delphy, 57
Carolina: East, 99; North, 6, 14, 15, 54, 99; South, 6, 12, 13, 14, 15, 54, 61–65, 71, 99
Cassell, John, 67, 68
Catch-up-a-Little, warship tender, 30
Cawley, Elizabeth Hoon (ed.), *The American Diaries of Richard Cobden* (1952), 77
Centralia, Ill., 90
Centurion, H.M.S., 99
Chapman, Mr. ——, 93, 94, 95
Charles II, King, 3
Charles Town, W.Va., 11
Charleston, S.C., 61–65
Charlestown, Mass., 20, 97
Chartists, 44
Chase Brothers & Co. of Boston, 62
Chase County, Kan., 45
Chatham, Lord, *see* Pitt, William.
Cherokee Indians, 11–13
Chesapeake, U.S.S., 26
Chesapeake Bay, blockade and invasion of, 26–31
Chicago, Ill., 77, 85, 89, 90
Chichester, Bishop of, 13
Chichester, Sussex, 34, 97–98, 103, 107
Chiltington, West, Sussex, 11
Cincinnati, Ohio, 77, 90
Civil War, 1861–65, 54–76, 101
Cobblestone buildings in N.Y., 106–107
Cobden: Frederick, 83; Henry, 78; Richard, 65–90, 101
Cobden Papers, 32, 39, 47–48, 50–53, 65–90
Cockburn, Admiral George, 26, 27
Codrington, Captain of the Fleet Edward, 29
Colden, Cadwallader, 10
Cole, E., 34
Collinson, Peter, 100
Colonization Society, 51
Colorado, 45, 105
Columbus, Christopher, 4
Common Sense, by Tom Paine (1776), 102
Concord, Mass., 19, 100
Coney Island, N.Y., 78
Confederate States of America, 54, 59, 61, 63, 73, 74, 87
Connéaut, Ohio, 81
Connecticut, 3, 15, 19, 99, 106
Connecticut Valley, 2
Coolham, Sussex, 98
Cork, County, Ireland, 35
Cotton, 66, 72–74, 75, 80
Cottonwood Valley, Kan., 45
Cowdray, Sussex, 35
Cowdray Archives, 35
Crick, B. R. and Miriam Alman and *Guide to Manuscripts Relating to America in Great Britain and Ireland* (1961), v
Cridland, F. J., 65
Crimean War, 72
Cromwell, Cato, 98

Cross Roads, N.J., 42
Cuckfield, Sussex, 32–33
Culpeper: Sir Edward, 97; Thomas, 2nd Lord, 97
Cumberland, Md., 79
Cyphering, 62, 65

Davis, Jefferson, 54, 87
De La Warr, Lord, *see* West, Thomas.
Dean, West, Archives, 20, 22, 98
Declaration of Independence, 22, 49, 51, 60, 102
Delaware: Bay, 97; colony/state of, 60, 97, 102, 105; Indians, 8; River, 2, 3, 97
Denalry, Michael and family, 35
Denny, William, 7–9
Detroit, Mich., 39
Diarists and the U.S.A., 77–96
Dicey, Edward, and *Six Months in the Federal States* (1863), 77
Dickens, Charles, and *American Notes* (1842), 77, 85, 86, 87
Ditchling, Sussex, 36–37, 43
Dough-faces, 71
Dougherty, Daniel, and *Fears for the Future of the Republic* (1859), 54–56
Dragon, H.M.S., 30
Drew, John, 98
Dubuque, Ia., 87–88
Dunford House, Heyshott, Sussex, 101
Dunleith, Ill., 87
Duquesne, Fort, Pa., 7
Dutch in America, the, 2–3
Dutch West India Company, 2, 3

East Carolina, *see* Carolina, East.
Eastern Penitentiary, Pa., 85
Easton, Pa., 8
Economy, Pa., 80
Edburton, Sussex, 98–99
Edge, F. M., 75
Effingham, Lord, *see* Howard, Thomas.
Egmont, Lord, *see* Perceval, George James.
Egremont, Earl of, *see* Wyndham, Sir Charles.
Egypt, 67
Eliot, George, and *Adam Bede* (1859), 94, 95
Emigrants' destinations: Boston, Mass., 97; Cross Roads, N.J., 42; Detroit, Mich., 39–40; Jamestown, Va., 1; Lysander, N.Y., 42–43; Peoria, Ill., 43–45; Pittsford, N.Y., 40–41
Emigrants from Ireland, 35, 80
Emigrants from London, England, 43–45
Emigrants from Sussex; *the names in italics indicate that further members of each emigrant family are named in the text:* Allin, Rev. John, v, 103; Bridger, Thomas, 34; Bristow, John, 36; Burgess, John, 43; *Grevatt, George,* 39–40; *Harvey, John,* 34, 42–43; Hunt, Rev. Robert, 101; Isted, William, 33; *Kimber, George,* 40–41; Merton, James, 34; Parsons, James, 35–36; Peachey, Joseph, 34; Pelham, Herbert, v, 101–102; *Pelham, Peter,* v, 97; Percy, George, v, 102; Sadler, Anne,

103; Smart, George, 34; Smart, Reuben, 34; *Southerton, Charles*, 33–34, 42; *Southerton, George*, 34; Tourle, William, 38; *Verrall, George*, 36–37; *White, George*, 34; Woodruff, Harriet, 34
Emigration, 32–48, 81
Emigration from Sussex: Aldingbourne, 33–34; Chichester, 97; Ditchling, 36–37, 43; Hastings, 100–101; Heathfield, 101; Horsted Keynes, 40–41; Lindfield (Scaynes Hill), 33; Ringmer, 103; Rye, v, 37, 103; Sullington, 39–40; West Grinstead, 35–36, 38
English language in America, 105
English pronunciation, archaic, in America, 105
Epreuve, H.M.S., 12
Erie, Lake, 7, 81
Everett, Edward, 57–59

Fain, Mrs. ——, 40
Fancy, steamboat, 80
Farragut, Captain (later Admiral) David, 76
Fauquier, Francis, 11–12
Fears for the Future of the Republic, by Daniel Dougherty (1859), 54–56
Felpham, Sussex, 99
Felton, C. C., 56
Fetherstonhaugh, Sir Matthew, 100
Firle, Sussex, 99–100
Fittleworth, Sussex, 77
Flint buildings in Sussex, 106–107
Florida, 5, 6, 15, 54
Forgery of emigrants' letters, 41
Frankfort, Me., 14
Frankland: Dame Agnes, 98; Charles Henry, 98
Franklin, Benjamin, 102
Frasch, Robert W., 106–107
Frederick, Md., 79
Frederick Town, Md., 27
Fredericksburg, VA., 98
Free Trade, 76, 101
French Communists (or Icarians), 44
French Revolution, 13–14, 73
Fuller Collection, 13, 14
Furs and skins, trade in, 16

Gage, General Thomas, 18, 19, 20, 97, 99–100
Garratt and Gibbon, Messrs., 34
Garrison, William Lloyd, 49, 51, 52
Gas, manufacture of, 75
Gentleman's Magazine, The, 12, 17–19, 21–22
George III, King, 11, 17, 20
George Town (Washington), D.C., 79
Georgia, 14, 15, 54, 75, 77, 90
German mercenary troops, 29
Gold rush, Pikes' Peak, 88–89
Goodwood, Sussex, 15, 100
Goodwood Archives, 7–9, 15–16, 20, 22–23, 32, 37
Goring, Mrs. Mary, 35–36
Governors, colonial, in America: Boone, Thomas, 13; Colden, Cadwallader, 10; Culpeper, Lord Thomas, 97; De La

Warr, Lord, v, 97; Denny, William, 7–9; Fauquier, Francis, 11–12; Gage, General Thomas, 18, 19, 20, 97, 99–100; Percy, George, v, 102; Sharpe, Horatio, 9; Shirley, William, 97, 102–103
Grand Ohio Company, vi, 100
Grattan: Henry, 88; Thomas Colley, and *Civilised America* (1859), 77
Gray, G., 34
Grevatt, George, 39–40
Grinstead, West, Sussex, 35–36, 39

Hagers Town, Md., 79
Hailsham, Sussex, 100
Halifax, Nova Scotia, 28, 85
Hall, Basil, 83
Hammond, James Henry, 71
Hampshire, England, 69, 97
Hampton, St. Simons Island, Ga., 94
Harlem, N.Y., 3, 22, 78
Harmony Society, 80
Harper's Ferry, Va., 57, 58, 61
Harting, South, Sussex, 100
Harvard, John, v, 103
Harvard University, 56, 66, 100, 103
Harvey, John and family, 34, 42–43
Harvey County, Kan., 45
Hasler, Richard, 34
Hastings, Sussex, 100–101, 107
Hastings, U.S.A. place name, 105
Hawkins Papers, 24–25
Haywards Heath, Sussex, 101
Heathfield, Sussex, 101
Henry, Patrick, 49, 88
Hessian mercenary troops, 22
Heyshott, Sussex, 67, 77, 101
Hickman, Ky., 86
Hoboken, N.Y., 82
Holly Spring[s], Miss., 87
Holmes, Oliver Wendell, and *Agnes*, 98
Homan, Thomas, 41
Homewood, William, 37
Hopkins, R. Thurston, and *Sussex Pilgrimages* (1927), 105
Hopkinton, Mass., 98
Hore, Henry, 98
Horsham, Pa., 105
Horsted Keynes, Sussex, 40, 41
Howard, Thomas, 3rd Earl of Effingham, 18
Hudson Valley, 2, 23
Humble, William, 4
Hunt, Rev. Robert, 101
Hunting expeditions in Georgia, 94–96
Hunting Town, Md., 27

Icarians (or French Communists), 44
Illinois, 43–44, 81, 90
Illinois Central Rail Road, 65, 77, 85, 87
Independence: Declaration of, 22, 49, 51, 60, 102; War of, v, 15, 17–23, 98, 99, 100
India and cotton, 72, 74
Indian, S.S., 90
Indiana, 80, 81
Indianapolis, Ind., 90
Indians, 1, 2, 6, 7–9, 14, 16, 23, 26, 46, 92, 100–101

Indies, West, 6, 79
Industrial Revolution (in Great Britain), 32
Ireland, 35, 80, 90
Irish potato famine, 1845 and 1846, 35
Isted, William, 33

James, Duke of York, 3
James, Henry, v, 103
Jamestown, Va., 1
Jan Cladpole's Trip to 'Merricur in Search of Dollar Trees, by Richard Lower (n.d.), 105
Jefferson, Thomas, 51, 76
Jenyns, Soame, 21
Jevington, Sussex, 40

Kansas, 45–47, 60
Keene, Henry, 100
Keith, Rev. George, 98–99
Kelly, J. Frederick, and *Early Domestic Architecture of Connecticut* (1963), 106
Kentucky, 74, 86
Kentucky Reporter, 50
Kimber, George and Jane, 40–41
King, William, 40
Kinsman, Ohio, 81
Kipling, Rudyard, 103
Knepp Castle, Shipley, Sussex, 35
Knyphausen, Lieutenant-General Wilhelm von, 22

Labrador, 90
Laird shipyards, 74
Lancashire, England, 66, 73
Lancaster, Pa., 8
Las Vegas, N.M., 45
Lavington, West, Sussex, 101
Lawley, Mr. ——, 44
Lee, General Robert E., 76
Leeds Castle, near Maidstone, England, 97
Lennox, family name of Dukes of Richmond: Charles, 2nd Duke, 100; Charles, 3rd Duke, 15, 22, 100; Charles, 5th Duke, 32
Leopard, H.M.S., 26
Lewes, Del., 102, 105
Lewes, Sussex, v, 101–102
Lexington, Mass., 19, 100
Lexington Advertiser & Western Monitor, 50
Liberator, The, 49, 51
Liberty, 35
Lincoln, Abraham, 53, 54, 56–57, 59, 66, 70, 74, 75, 76
Lincoln, England, 90
Lindfield, Sussex, 33, 37, 101
Little John, warship tender, 30
Little St. Simons Island, Ga., 94
Liverpool, England, 35, 37, 75, 83, 85, 89, 91
Lohort Castle estate, County Cork, Ireland, 35
London, England, 4, 10, 11, 12, 13, 18, 20, 22, 38, 43, 44, 45, 46, 70, 78, 89
London Gazette, The, 19
London Packet, The (or *New Lloyd's Evening Post*), 22

Long Island, N.Y., 22, 78, 99
Loudon, Lord, *see* Campbell, John.
Louisiana, 26, 54, 67, 75
Lowell, Mass., 82
Lower, Richard, and *Jan Cladpole's Trip to 'Merricur in Search of Dollar Trees* (n.d.), 105
Lucas, Samuel, 66
Luddites, 32
Lyminster, Sussex, 14
Lyons, Richard Bickerton Pemell, 2nd Baron and 1st Earl Lyons, 49, 56, 57, 61, 64, 65, 66
Lyons Papers, v, 49, 54–65
Lysander, N.Y., 42

Machinery, a social problem in England, 32
Mackay, Alexander, and *Western World* (1849), 77
Maitland and Phelps, New York, 91
Malling, South, Sussex, 103
Manchester, England, 67, 82
Manhattan Island, N.Y., 2
Manhattan-ville, N.Y., 78
Marblehead, Mass., 98
Marion County, Kan., 45
Marlborough, Mass., 19
[Marlborough], Malborough, Md: Lower, 28, 29; Upper, 28, 29
Marsh, Thomas W., and *Some Records of the Early Friends in Surrey and Sussex . . .* (1886), 104
Martineau, Harriet, and *Society in America* (1836) and *A Retrospect of Western Travel* (1838), 77
Maryland, 1, 6, 9, 15, 59–61, 79, 104, 105
Maryland Committee on Federal Relations, 59–61
Mason, R. T., and *Framed Buildings of the Weald* (2nd edn. 1969), 106
Massachusetts, 15, 17, 19, 51, 70, 76, 98, 99, 102, 103
Massachusetts Company, 100
Mather, Rev. Increase, 13
Mattoon, Ill., 90
Maxse: Frederick Augustus, 96; Frederick Ivor, 77, 90–96
Maxse Papers, 90–96
Mayflower Compact, 1
McClellan, George B., 85
McHenry, Fort, Md., 29
Memphis, Tenn., 85, 86, 90
Mennonites, 45
Mercenary troops, German, 29
Meredith, George, and *Beauchamp's Career* (1876), 96
Merton, James, 34
Mesopotamia, 67
Mexico, 73
Mexico, Gulf of, 67
Michigan, 81
Midhurst, Sussex, 67, 68, 69
Millyard, Charles, 34
Minneapolis, Minn., 77
Minnesota, 105
Mississippi, 54, 67, 87

Mississippi, River, 6, 7, 44, 47, 55, 67, 77, 79, 85, 86, 87, 89, 90
Mississippian & Natchez Advertiser, The, 50
Missouri, 60
Missouri, River, 88
Mobile, Ala., 73
Molasses, trade in, 16
Monroe, Ohio, 81
Monrow [Monroe] County, N.Y., 41
Montreal, Canada, 90
Morrill Tariff Act, 1861, 68
Murfee, Eleanor, 40
Murser, Dame ——, 40

Napoleon I, Emperor, 26
Narrangansett Indians, 100
National Archives, Washington, D.C., 22
Navoo [Nauvoo], Ill., 44
Nebraska, 105
New Amsterdam [New York], 2, 3
New Brighton, Minn. and Pa., 105
New Brunswick, N.J., 42
New England, 1, 2, 5, 14, 23, 26, 68, 71, 100, 102
New England College, vi
New Hampshire, 15
New Harmony, Ind., 80
New Jersey, 3, 6, 14, 15, 42, 49, 98–99, 103, 105
New Mexico, 45
New Netherland, 2–3
New Orleans, La., 26, 51, 63, 73, 86
New York, city, 3, 14, 15, 18, 22, 33, 34, 35, 39, 44, 46, 47–48, 49, 51, 54, 57, 67, 69, 74, 75, 78, 81, 82, 83, 85, 89–90, 91, 96, 100, 103, 105
New York, colony/state of, 3, 6, 8, 10, 14, 32, 40, 41, 42, 49, 98, 99, 106, 107
New York Association for the Improvement of the Condition of the Poor, 47
New York City Almshouse Commissioners, 47
New York Magdalen Female Benevolent Society, 47
Newfoundland, 14
Newport, R.I., 97
Niagara Falls, 81–82, 85
Niagara, Fort, N.Y., 7
Niantic Indians, 100–101
Norfolk, England, 90
North Carolina, *see* Carolina, North.
Norton, Sallie, 103
Nottingham, Md., 27, 28
Nottinghamshire, England, 90
Nourse, Captain J., 26
Nova Scotia, 14, 15, 85

Oakecharinga Tiggwawtubby Tocholochy Yuca, 11
Ockenden, Thomas, 41
Ohio, 80, 81
Ohio, River, 7, 80, 86
Open Air Museum, Singleton, Sussex, 106
Osborn, W. H., 65, 67, 69, 74, 85
Ovingdean, Sussex, 107
Owen: Robert, 80; William, 34

Paine, Tom, 101–102
Palmerston, Lord, *see* Temple, Henry John.
Paris, Treaties of: 1763, 6, 15; 1783, 24
Parish, Rev. W. D., and *Dictionary of the Sussex Dialect . . .* (1875), 105
Parsons, James, 35–36
Patuxent, River, 26, 29
Peachey, Joseph, 34
Pelham: Henry, 20, 97–98; Herbert, v, 100–101; Peter, v, 97
Penn: Laetitia, 98; Thomas, 7; William, v, 7, 13, 98, 103, 104
Pennsylvania, v, 6, 7–9, 14, 15, 68, 80, 98, 99, 104, 105
Peoria, Ill., 43–44
Perceval, George James, 6th Earl of Egmont, 35
Percy, George, v, 102
Petworth, Sussex, 41, 102
Petworth House, Sussex, vi, 9, 102
Petworth House Archives, v, vi, 2–3, 9–13, 102
Philadelphia, Pa., 7–9, 14, 17, 22, 44, 52, 57, 75, 78, 90, 98, 100, 102
Pickering, Arthur, 70
Pilgrim Fathers, 1
Pikes' Peak gold rush, 88–89
Pitt William, 1st Earl of Chatham, 23
Pittsburgh, Pa., 80, 81
Pittsford, N.Y., 40, 41
Place names, Sussex, in U.S.A., 105
Plumly, Major B. Rush, 51–53
Plymouth Plantation, Mass., 1
Poland, Ohio, 81
Poor Law Commissioners, 42
Portsmouth, England, 12, 26, 29, 33, 34, 37
Potomac, River, 27, 63
Potter, Thomas B., 67, 70
Potters Emigration Society, 44
Poverty in 19th century Sussex, 32–33
Preston, Sussex, 102–103
Prior, George, 34
Prospect of the Most Famous Parts of the World, A, (1646), 4–5
Protection, fiscal policy of, 68
Providence, R.I., 15
Provisions: prices of in Sussex, 32–33; U.S.A., 39, 41, 42, 43
Puritans, 1, 13, 103
Pyles, Thomas, and *Words and Ways of American English* (1954), 105

Quakers, 7–9, 98–99, 101, 104
Quebec, Canada, 17, 90
Quincy, Ill., 44

Railways, 45, 65, 72, 75, 77, 82, 85, 87, 90
Raleigh, Sir Walter, 5
Raleigh, N.C., 62
Rapp, George, 80
Rappahannock, Va., 29
Rational Society, Congress of the, 80
Rhode Island, vi, 15, 97, 99
Richmond, Dukes of, *see* under Lennox.
Richmond, Va., 63, 65, 76, 96
Richmond Fort, 14
Ridge &c., Messrs., Chichester, 34

Ringmer, Sussex, 103
Robespierre, Maximilien, 76
Rochester, N.Y., 106
Rocky Mountains, 47, 79, 88
Roosevelt family, 3
Ross, Dr. Alexander Milton, 63
Ross, Major-General Robert, 28
Rottingdean, Sussex, 103, 107
Royal Ark, H.M.S., 28
Royal Sussex Regiment, 98
Roxbury, West, Mass., 76
Rum, trade in, 16
Russell: Lord John, 1st Earl Russell, 66;
    Dr. William Howard, 71
Russia, 72
Rye, N.Y., 103, 105
Rye, Sussex, v, 37, 103

Sadler, Anne, 103
Sale, [?William], 90
Salem, Mass., 18, 19
Sandhurst, Royal Military College, England, 77, 90
Sante Fe, N.M., 45
Saratoga, N.Y., 23
Saratoga Springs, N.Y., 49
Savannah, Ga., 92, 96
Scaines [Scaynes] Hill, Lindfield, Sussex, 33
Secession, 54, 56, 61, 63, 70, 72
Sedlescombe, Sussex, 106
Severn, H.M.S., 26, 29
Seward, William H., 54
Sharpe, Horatio, 9
Shipley, Sussex, 35
Shirley: Cecily, 97; Sir Thomas, 97; William, 97, 102–103
Shoreham, Vt., 105
Short, Henry, 36
Singleton, Open Air Museum at, Sussex, 106
Skiagusta Ocenesta, 11
Slave States of the Border, 60
Slavery, 26, 49–53, 54, 56, 57–59, 62, 66–67, 68–70, 73–75, 76, 79, 80, 81, 86, 87
Smart: George, 34; Reuben, 34
Smith, Francis Key, 29
Smith, J. B., 73
Society for the Propagation of the Gospel in Foreign Parts, 13–14, 98–99
Sockett, Rev. T., 41
South: *see* Carolina; Harting; Malling.
Southern Virginia, *see* Virginia, Southern.
Southerton: Charles and family, 33–34, 42; George and family, 34
Sowton and Fuller, Messrs., 34
Springett: Guilelma Maria, 103; Sir William, 103
Squier, E. G., and *Is Cotton "King"?: Sources of Cotton Supply* (1861), 72
St. [San] Francisco, Cal. 89, 103
St. George's Society of New York, 47–48
St. Louis, Mo., 44, 77, 88–89
St. Paul, Minn., 77
St. Simons Island, Ga., 90, 92–96
Staplefield, Sussex, 102, 104
'Star Spangled Banner', 29

Stars and Bars, the, 54
Staten Island, N.Y., 83
Steevens, George Warrington, and *The Land of the Dollar* (1898), 77
Steyning, Sussex, 104
Storrington, Sussex, 36
Stowe, Harriet Beecher, and *Uncle Tom's Cabin* (1852), 51
Stuyvesant, Peter, 3
Sugar, 75
Sullington, Sussex, 39, 40
Sumner, Charles, 66, 70
Sumter, Fort, S.C., 63–65, 76
Sussex and America, 97–107
Sussex Americanisms, 105
Sussex County Magazine, v, 43, 97, 98, 100, 101, 102, 103, 104, 106
Sussex dialect, 105
Sussex place names in U.S.A., 105
Swing, Captain, riots, 32

Tarring, West, Sussex, 107
Teedyuscung, Chief, 8
Temple, Henry John, 3rd Viscount Palmerston, 66
Tennessee, 54, 76
Texas, 44, 54
Timber-framed buildings in England and U.S.A., 106
Times, The, 24–25
Timothy the tortoise, 103
Tobacco, 2, 27, 86
Tocqueville, Alexis de, and *Democracy in America* (1835–40), 70
Tonnant, H.M.S., 28
Tourle, William, 38
Trade, 18th century restrictions on American, 15–16
Trafalgar, Battle of, 26
Trent incident, 1861, 66
Trollope, Mrs. Frances, and *Domestic Manners of the Americans* (1832), 77, 83
Tucker, Josiah, 21
Tuskeestannagee Whosly Powon Micco, 11

Uncle Tom's Cabin, by Harriet Beecher Stowe (1852), 51
'Underground railroad', 52–53
Union[town], Pa., 79
United Provinces, 20
Uppark, Sussex, 100

Van Cortlandt, Colonel Philip, 100
Vandalia, projected colony of, W.Va., 100
Vandalia, tower of, South Harting, Sussex, 100
Vanderbilt family, 3
Vermont, 49, 105
Verrall: George and Harriet, 36–37; Walter, 36–37
Vesputius, Americus [Amerigo Vespucci], 4
Virginia, v, 1, 2, 5, 6, 11, 13, 15, 54, 61, 97, 99, 102, 103, 104, 105, 106
Virginia, Southern, 99
Virginia, Western, 39, 100

Virginian Assembly, 1
Visscher, Nicolas, 2

Wages: level of in Sussex, 32–33, 39, 42;
    in U.S.A., 39–40, 41, 42, 43, 80
Wakehurst Place, Ardingly, Sussex, 97
Wales, Prince of, 72
War Eagle, steamboat, 88
War of Independence, v, 15, 17–23, 98, 99,
    100
War of 1812–1814, 26–31
Warminghurst, Sussex, 98, 104
Washington: George, v, 22, 24–25, 51, 76,
    102, 104; John, 104; Lawrence, 104;
    family in Petworth, Sussex, 102
Washington, D.C., 22, 26, 29, 49, 56, 61,
    64, 66, 70, 79, 90, 96
Washington, Fort (or Fort Knyphausen),
    Pa., 22
Washington, Sussex, 41
Wealden Buildings Study Group, 106
Welcome, sailing ship, 104
West, Thomas, 3rd Baron De La Warr, v,
    97
West: *see* Chiltington; Dean; Grinstead;
    Indies; Lavington; Roxbury; Tarring.
Western Virginia, *see* Virginia, Western.
Wherwell, England, 97
White, George, and family, 34
White, Gilbert, 103

White-Hall Evening Post, 20
White Plains, Battle of, 98
Whitefield, Rev. George, 13
Whitney's cotton gin, 49
Whyte's, J. B., *General Provision Warehouse*,
    38
Wilde, Oscar, 96
William Henry, Fort, N.Y., 8
William Penn, steamboat, 81
Williamsburg, Va., 11
Wilsone, Dr. ——, 82
Winchester, England, 12
Wisconsin, 44, 105
Wiston House, Sussex, 97
Wiston Park, Sussex, 35
Withyham, Sussex, 97
Woodbridge, N.J., 103
Woodruff, Harriet, 34
Woods, Mrs. ——, 40
Woodward, Rev. W. P., 35–36
Worthing, Sussex, 107
Wyndham, Sir Charles, 2nd Earl of Egre-
    mont, 9–13
Wyoming, 105
Wyoming, steam packet, 91

Yorkshire, England, 90
Young, Rev. Arthur, and *General View of
    the Agriculture of the County of Sussex* (1808),
    32–33

PRINTED BY MOORE AND TILLYER AT THE REGNUM PRESS, CHICHESTER